What

It

Means

to

Write

What
It
Means
to
Write

Creativity and Metaphor

ADRIAN McKERRACHER

McGILL-QUEEN'S UNIVERSITY PRESS

Montreal & Kingston · London · Chicago

ISBN 978-0-7735-5633-1 (cloth)
ISBN 978-0-7735-5721-5 (ePDF)
ISBN 978-0-7735-5722-2 (ePUB)

Legal deposit first quarter 2019
Bibliothèque nationale du Québec

Printed in Canada on acid-free paper that is 100% ancient forest free
(100% post-consumer recycled), processed chlorine free

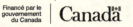

Funded by the   Financé par le
Government   gouvernement
of Canada   du Canada

Canada Council   Conseil des arts
for the Arts   du Canada

We acknowledge the support of the Canada Council for the Arts, which
last year invested $153 million to bring the arts to Canadians throughout
the country.

Nous remercions le Conseil des arts du Canada de son soutien. L'an
dernier, le Conseil a investi 153 millions de dollars pour mettre de l'art
dans la vie des Canadiennes et des Canadiens de tout le pays.

Library and Archives Canada Cataloguing in Publication

McKerracher, Adrian, 1981–, author
What it means to write : creativity and metaphor / Adrian McKerracher.

Includes bibliographical references and index.
Issued in print and electronic formats.
ISBN 978-0-7735-5633-1 (cloth).
–ISBN 978-0-7735-5721-5 (ePDF).
–ISBN 978-0-7735-5722-2 (ePUB)

1. Metaphor. 2. Creative writing. 3. Creative ability. 4. Creation
(Literary, artistic, etc.). I. Title.

PN228.M4M35 2019   808'.032   C2018-905902-8

For my brother, who travels with me everywhere

Contents

What
It
Means
to
Write

Introduction

It was supposed to be a simple semester abroad at the University of Havana in Cuba. It was 2003. I would be there for three months, taking classes at the Faculty of Social Sciences and Humanities. The program was pleasant but predictable, the usual tour of a sanitized curriculum. Maybe it was no surprise that I began to lose interest. Or maybe I was there for another reason.

Soon enough I started skipping class to go on long walks through the city. From a bird's eye view my route would have looked aimless, but I was searching for something. A secret project had taken hold. I repeated my mission to anyone who would listen, asking at bookstores, museums, cafés, on sidewalks, in parks, theatre lobbies, and during musical intermissions. It became a mantra, something I turned to in the inevitable moments of self-doubt that haunt months away from home, when I wondered what I was doing. During those mornings, those days, those nights, when nothing seemed to hold the trip together, I remembered my private purpose and time rallied in a rush of hope – not only hope for the future, where hope was usually found, but for the present, where hope was lifting me up. I wasn't there for the classes or the music or the political history, although I was willing to use any of them to reach my goal.

I was there to meet writers.

I went to publishing houses and literary talks and libraries, describing my quest to anyone who would listen. By chance, after attending half a dozen book launches, smiling dopily at strangers, shaking hands, beaming at the glimpses of community, I found myself face to face with the president of the Writers and Artists Union of Cuba. He had enormous hands and the rugged face of a bear. I stammered my mantra.

I'm here to meet writers.

Yes yes, fine, he said, and passed me off to someone he said was the editor of a literary magazine. That man said the same thing, yes yes, fine. Then he gave me a piece of paper with a number on it.

Call this woman, he said. She can help.

I called, waiting so long in the hot sun of the phone booth that sweat poured down my neck, the phone ringing into the void, until a woman answered breathlessly, as if she had been running up a flight of stairs.

I'm from Canada, I said, and I'm here to meet writers.

Look, she said. I don't have time to talk right now. But come to this address at eleven o'clock on Thursday morning.

Then she hung up.

The place was in Old Havana, a bell tower with a little bookstore tucked into the ground floor and a pile of stairs at the back. I followed a man who I decided was a writer. He had a lean, gentle face with a thin beard, stooped posture, wearing a bland shirt tucked into his jeans, and he carried a book under his arm. We passed moss-covered rooms filled with broken chairs. I lost sight of him and followed the sound of his shoes on the stones until I reached the tower where the bell would have been a long time ago. In its place was a table with eight people seated around it. A freckled woman turned and looked at me.

You must be Adrian, she said. It was the woman from the phone.

I'm Reina María Rodríguez. Sit down. We're starting.

As luck would have it, this was the place where some of the most prized writers in Havana met every week to give talks to one another about some aspect of their work. That day a playwright was presenting on the challenges of translating a script set in rural France into a bucolic Cuban dialect.

A farm in France doesn't sound like a farm in Cuba, the playwright explained, but somehow they are the same farm.

The bell tower was affectionately called *La Torre de Libros* – The Tower of Books. For the next two months, I skipped class every Thursday to join these sessions. Soon I asked the writers if I could meet them in their homes. I had hardly read any of their books but I wanted to know about their lives. I wanted to know how they felt about converting thoughts into words. I visited them with a tape recorder and a bottle of wine and asked questions that were naive when written down but out loud were sincere: Where do ideas come from? How do you know when a paragraph is good? Is there such a thing as fiction? One conversation with the novelist and playwright Antón Arrufat stood out: citing his friend the late Virgilio Piñera, he explained that a writer must learn not only how to hear himself but also how to write himself.

I adored the writers that I met in Havana. I wanted to be them, to talk the way they talked and know what they knew. But it wasn't simply worship. It was research. I wanted to know what it meant to be creative.

I had wondered this for years. Back in Canada, I hosted a community radio show called the "Creative Experience" at CHMA 106.9 FM in New Brunswick about the lives of artists: why writers wrote, what it meant to paint, what happened when people sang. Before that, when I was much younger, I idolized Walter Elias Disney – the man, not the empire or the tantrums – because he had found a way to make a living from his imagination. He had invented a world in his mind that eventually came to inhabit this world. He was living by his creativity.

But beneath any research on what that word meant was a question that swam like a dark and terrible fish. It had the power to overturn me and leave me to drown in the wide space of mediocrity: *Was I a creative person?*

What if I couldn't do anything original? I wondered. What if my most personal act turned out to be banal? What if I was nothing like my heroes? What if I put my life into art and people rejected it, found it cliché, pat, conventional, dull, done before? What if I had nothing unique to offer and it was just me, another me, a me among the billions, winking into oblivion with no spark to illuminate even the little patch of life I inhabited? What if I didn't have the strength to carry out my ideas – what if I was too weak to deliver my own thoughts? And what if, once delivered, those thoughts turned out to be ugly? They would be out, I would wish they had never happened or that I had treated them better, but by then it would be too late.

No, it was better to look in on the lives of others than to confront my own. I would keep asking questions, keep reading, keep walking. The semester in Havana continued. I smoked cigars on rooftops and drank rum on the Malecón. I travelled with a theatre troupe and paid a magician to teach me sleight-of-hand tricks. I cut out pop-up books for the publishing house Ediciones Vijía. I wrote an audacious essay about the new generation of *trovadores* and their music. I went home to Canada and played parts of the interviews on the radio. Time passed. But the question didn't go away.

~

What Is Writing? What Is Creativity?

An advertisement for a college degree invites prospective students to unleash their creativity. A condominium real-estate agent insists that living in a particular building will celebrate a creative lifestyle. People staggering into the job market are told that employers want creative problem solvers, people who think outside the box. Couples trapped in stalemate are counselled to get creative with date night. Writers are encouraged to be creative with character and plot. It seemed that creativity had become a market commodity, adding value simply by being declared. It was an unimpeachable virtue, an unquestioned benevolent descriptor. I had never heard of someone complaining that an idea, a place, or a person was "too creative." But what did "creative" even mean?

I had the idea for this book while I was writing a story about my time in Havana. In fact, it was more accurate to say it was the *absence* of an idea that launched this book. I was recounting a day when a man had tried to sell me marijuana. He had befriended me in a park and led me all over the city. We had a good conversation. Then suddenly I was cornered by a friend of his who insisted I buy a joint. When I hesitated, the man grew angry.

Every tourist wants to smoke, he said. What's wrong with you?

I sputtered something, probably my mantra, and fled.

It took a long time to write the story. Even though I knew what happened, I couldn't get it right. Sometimes the man who had befriended me came out like a villain; sometimes the villain was me. After multiple attempts, when there was no clear path through the story, I gave up. I had writer's block.

Writer's block. What a curious image. I saw the act of writing as a journey, trying to get from A to B, and there was an obstacle in the way. Or maybe it was a pipe with something lodged in it, inhibiting the flow. Either way, it presumed a spatial map of the problem, one that demanded movement, and the thwarted desire to leave one place behind and arrive someplace else. The blank page was the origin; the story was the destination. I was stuck, not getting anywhere, things weren't moving along. Did it have to be that way?

I tried to think of the experience in other terms. What about music, I wondered. Maybe not being able to write was akin to a rest, a pause in the larger work that was still part of its complete form. I wasn't stuck. I just wasn't playing a note at that moment. Or maybe this was a coda, an invitation to loop back to the beginning and start again, knowing what was ahead. Or maybe the problem was a matter of tuning.

I thought of other images to explain what had happened. Not being able to write was a dark cloud. All I could do was wait for it to pass. Not being able to write was a bully that said I wasn't good enough. I made deals with it, trying to buy it off with other errands. Not being able to write was a gift. I should accept it and play outside.

So this would be my return to the question that hadn't left me. I would set out in search of metaphors for creativity. Each one would nuance my understanding of what it meant to be creative. With time I began to notice metaphors everywhere. When someone said they felt "inspired," they invoked an ancient Greek perspective that creativity was possession by one of nine muses who breathed life – literally "to inspire" – into the artist so that they could manifest their work.[1] When Ernest Hemingway (1899–1961) wrote how important it was "to not think about anything [he] was writing from the time [he] stopped writing until [he] started again the next day,"[2] he implied the metaphor that creativity was a process of incubation, putting ideas aside to be worked out unconsciously before being revisited.[3] More recently, when the late Steve Jobs (1955–2011) observed that creative people "just saw something different,"[4] he hinted at a metaphor of illumination, whereby new insight into a project was revealed through challenging conventional perspectives. And there were others, many others.

I was not trying to determine a singular, dominant metaphor. I wanted to explore the range of what was possible, always asking how it could be otherwise. It would be a kind of literacy, reading the significance of creativity by the metaphors people used to describe it. And maybe, just maybe, I would learn what the word meant to me and why it had such haunting, troubling, exciting power.

I already knew where I needed to go. It wasn't Havana.

~

The seed of Buenos Aires was planted in my imagination when, during my teenage years on the west coast of Canada, the first person I kissed ended our tryst with a gift. It was a collection of short stories by Jorge Luis Borges. Suffused with labyrinths and mirrors, the book was a riddle I used as distraction during the long summer apart. Inside the cover she had written, "I'll think of you when it rains."

A year later, when I finished high school, I went to Chile to volunteer at a music school. I set up benches for the choir's performances and dabbled in percussion, then hitchhiked to the south with a dear friend. At night, next to campfires and under stars, we drank wine, wrote in our journals, and talked about the world, which was ours. The idea of Buenos Aires glowed brighter next to that long thin country, in the form of movies, TV shows, music, and some news, but I didn't know then that it would one day transform me.

Back in my Canadian life, something was missing. I found it in *Hopscotch*, the wild novel by Julio Cortázar. The first page served as a kind of personality test. A Table of Instructions began: "In its own way, this book consists of many books, but two books above all."[5] It proceeded to outline the ways of reading, either in a consecutive, conventional fashion, or in a jumping (hence the title), non-linear order. I had heard of seminars that invited students to read any three chapters, at random, each week and discuss the collaborative way in which the meaning of a text is negotiated. I returned to the book again and again, unsure whether I was just starting or just finishing. The scale of the story seemed always to be expanding. How had I not known that books could be written like this? Here was the sense of mystery, possibility, experimentation, and wry humour I had craved. If I had to choose one book that made me want to write, it was that one.

I began to read my way up and down the continent and later travelled in Bolivia, Venezuela, Colombia, and Nicaragua. Over time, Buenos Aires shrank in comparison with the world, fading to a collection of sounds, a pair of words to mark a place on a map but not yet a reservoir of feelings. It came in and out of my life around the name of a co-worker or a bottle of wine. Otherwise I forgot about it. Years passed: school, work, questions about how and where to live. On a bike trip with my dad, camped by a river in Washington

State, I confessed to feeling lost. He reminded me of how excited I had been when I was meeting writers. Maybe there was something there. Within a year I was on a plane to Buenos Aires.

Borges and Cortázar, dated references as they were, the former born in 1899 and the latter in 1914, had lit a candle of hope for me in that distant South American city. With its reputation for nostalgia, melancholy, solidarity, and creativity, Buenos Aires wasn't just a place, it was a mood, and that mood was literary. People had been saying it for decades. Some speculated that the cultural productivity of the city was due to massive waves of immigration in the nineteenth and twentieth centuries. In 1910, for example, although most plays were in Spanish, there were also 400 plays in Italian, more than 100 plays in French, and many in Yiddish. In that year alone three million theatre tickets were sold.[6] When Christopher Isherwood visited Buenos Aires in 1948, he called it "the most truly international city in the world."[7] Carlos Fuentes, who lived in Buenos Aires when he was sixteen, described it, "then, as always, the most beautiful, sophisticated, and civilized city in Latin America."[8] Of course, not everyone adored it. The French architect Le Corbusier lectured that "Buenos Aires is the most inhumane city I've known. In fact, one's heart feels martyred there."[9] Disparaging reviews aside, the literary production was exceptional. Argentine literature was "one of the most prolific, relevant and influential in Latin America,"[10] and from 1940 to 1960 Buenos Aires was the centre of Spanish-language publishing worldwide.[11] In 2001 the Argentine government introduced the Ley del Fomento del Libro y la Lectura[12] (the Act to Promote Books and Reading), which provided subsidies to support publishing and reading, and afterwards the municipality of Buenos Aires passed a law that allowed writers over sixty years old to apply for a pension.[13] When the city was designated a UNESCO World Book Capital in 2011, there were more books sold per capita there than in any other city in the world.[14] Coupled with bookstores that stayed open until three o'clock in the morning and dozens of salons and workshops on any given night, there was no more literary milieu than Buenos Aires. There I would find my writers and discover what it meant to be creative. And I would do it in Spanish.

~

Spanish was my second language. In chronological terms it was my third, having stumbled through French lessons in rural west coast Canadian classrooms where *la belle langue* had little traction beyond the curriculum (by high school I had memorized some vegetables and certain rooms of a house), which paved the way for Spanish to overtake it. Still, the words were slow to move at first. I was just a teenager when I went to volunteer at the music school in Copiapó, Chile, a mining town later famous for the thirty-three miners trapped for over two months underground. When I arrived I was unable to make a sentence. All I could do was act things out, draw pictures, and plead with my eyes. My head leaned heavily against the window of the bus as I went home exhausted each day. Without language, I was lonely.

It's strange to me now that I never studied Spanish when I was there or even since, not in any formal way. I didn't take a class or look up rules or have a textbook. About three weeks into my time in Chile I spent an afternoon writing down conjugations of verb endings. That was it. Everything else I learned from listening and from speaking. That didn't mean I wasn't rigorous or systematic. When I noticed a pattern of speech, I marked it in my thoughts and listened for other instances. Entire monologues were distilled into a single verb tense, introductions to multiple generations of a family became no more than the placement of formal address. By the time I had heard a particular arrangement of language three times – I thought of them as shapes – I considered it sufficiently tested and the next instance was my responsibility. I had to use it myself. In an average day I was scanning for five or six of these language shapes, ready to confirm or revise them so that I could move on to another set. When the time came, I spoke and then waited. It was a peculiar thing, learning a language from scratch. Success was when no one noticed how much I had risked.

Since those first days at the music school, Spanish was an embodied language – I felt it in my mouth and in my hands, in my eyebrows and in my cheeks, in my shoulders and in my back. It was inseparable from the people I shared it with. There was no book between us, no rules. Learning French in a classroom, I had wanted to make a sentence. Learning Spanish in Chile, I wanted to make a friend.

After a month, I was surprised one afternoon when I told someone about my loneliness – surprised because I was telling them in Spanish. A couple of weeks later I was invited to a concert and then to parties in the desert. At the end of the semester I went camping on the beach with the graduating class, where we ended up in our underwear playing spin the bottle at 4 a.m. I went to church. I went to Bolivia. I had dreams in which my family spoke Spanish. I even had dreams I could write it.

As a Canadian of Scottish-English heritage, my whiteness meant that I could more or less blend in as a European immigrant. It also afforded me the privilege of an assumed upper class. My accent was the only thing that betrayed my foreigner status. Once, while travelling in Venezuela, I was asked if I was Costa Rican. In Chile I was asked if I had lived in Bolivia. In Cuba I was asked if I had family in South America (I don't). In Mexico I was asked if my parents were Latino (they are not). My Spanish was a puzzle, always from somewhere else. Then one day, an Argentine asked which part of Argentina I was from.

But all of that was backstory. The meaning of writing and creativity was up ahead, in the city that would quietly break me open. Hurry now, they're calling the gate, the plane is about to leave. You have all you need to get started. In fact, you have more than enough. I'll explain the rest on the way.

~

A Preliminary Survey of Metaphors for Creativity

During the flight to Buenos Aires I emptied my mind of English, shaking out the pockets of my thoughts for coins of a language that would soon have no value. I would live in Spanish for as long as I was away – speaking, listening, reading, and writing. The consequence of breaking my self-imposed rule was diffused and abstract, but real: every word in English belonged to a different system, one that drew farther away as the plane trailed south.

When I wasn't thinking of language in economic terms – its value, its circulation, the way some words took time to appreciate – I thought of it as though it were hanging in the air around the people who used it, like tiny lights hung from a tree, so that when I wanted to speak all I had to do was pluck the right words and return them to the person I was talking to, not necessarily their own words, but the ambient words we shared, little beacons of community. It was also why books were so important: reading was a well-lit tree full of words, showing the best of what language could do. It meant I could speak a language only when I was close to it. I had to see the lights. I had to reach them myself. Sometimes I felt embarrassed to tell people that I spoke Spanish because if asked in English I couldn't remember a word of it. Forsaking English was necessary, yet for the first half of the flight my mind was the empty space between two languages.

But not entirely empty. A few words rolled around on the floor of my thoughts, some in English, and then gradually, some in Spanish. Later more Spanish words arrived over the seats of the plane and along the aisle, then in hushed voices between the elderly couple who muttered nearby, just loud enough to make out the texture of the sounds but not the meaning. At times a fully formed Spanish word appeared in the air, from the loudspeaker, explaining the altitude or the schedule of meals. I collected those words as if I were putting them in a little purse, the same one I had filled on other trips and reluctantly emptied each time I came back to English.

Because I had renounced my first language, none of the Spanish words were tethered to any counterpart in English. If they had a partner it was the accumulated experiences I had had of that word, a personal history of language. Trading one word for another as if they were equivalent would have meant working through two languages at once while navigating the mysterious space between them, the space of translation, which was a separate language altogether. Instead, the Spanish words had their own life, their own light, although that light was erratic, at times wild and bright and other times dull, compared to the English words that I had given up. The problem was just that I had fewer of them.

The plane engine droned. I looked at the clouds.

For most of the flight, the Spanish I accumulated was a random mix of discrete objects –new words but not new shapes. I repeated them one at a time, coming back to them like a lumbering brute, ready to make something but not knowing what. Then a woman in the seat ahead turned to the person beside her and said, *Casi llegamos*. It was a banal phrase, common and plain, something like "we're almost there" or, more precisely, "almost we arrive," but at the same time it was entirely different from anything English could express, not just because of the sounds and the syntax but because of its history. It had a place that was all its own in hundreds of years of speaking. If it had anything in common with "we're almost there," it was that people tended to use these expressions in similar circumstances. Hearing the phrase folded the pocket of my mind inside out. Where I was going was more than words.

~

*"Región de la aurora! ¡Oh, tierra abierta al sediento de libertad
y de vida, dinámica y creadora!"*
Region of the aurora! Oh, land open to those thirsty for
liberty and for life, dynamic and creative!

That's what visionary modernist Nicaraguan poet Rubén Darío
wrote about Argentina in his *Canto a la Argentina* in 1910. I would
find out if it were still true more than a century later, when my
plane touched down at Ezeiza Airport and a man with the sad jowls
of a walrus led me from the taxi stand to one of the cars outside. I
asked him how his day was going and commented on the breeze.
He muttered something as if the words were dribbling down his
chin. At the other side of the parking lot he handed a pink slip of
paper to one of the drivers. When I climbed into the back seat, he
spat on the ground where I had stood. Was it already obvious that
I didn't belong?

As we sped along the highway into Buenos Aires, the driver and
I talked enough to demonstrate that we were people with lives. The
aura of his family, his wife and his two kids, softened the edges of
his face and turned his big, hard hands into nothing more than the
tools he used to eat his breakfast and drive this car. I went quiet. I
looked out the window at the buildings and the billboards that
lined the highway. I had the sensation that the city was appearing
just for me, assembling seconds before I arrived and collapsing as
soon as I passed, so that it needed me to exist. I thought of my dad
and his humbler vision of travel: he believed that we left a candle
burning each place we went, illuminating our memories of that
place, so that our path through the world was lit by nodes of light.

Through the window of the taxi, the city looked familiar even
though I had never been there before – the apartments, the offices,
the grey light of the sky. It was as if a candle were already burning.

We exited the highway and lowered suddenly into the neighbourhood of Constitución. I snapped back into my body, bracing
to meet the city. The area where I was staying had a reputation

for violence and crime, an opinion that my host would vehemently reject.

Acá estamos, said the driver, pulling over. Here we are.

Suddenly I was out, resenting my luggage not for its weight but for its proof that I wasn't from here. The taxi drove away, leaving the myths and realities of Buenos Aires stretching out in every direction. I crossed the street through the blue smoke of exhaust to the house number I had been given and knocked at the door. The deadbolt clanged. Eugenio, the father of a friend and the man I would live with, peered through a shadowy crack, a wisp of white hair hanging over the armadillo skin of his forehead, the lines of his face arranging around a toothy smile.

I'm Adrian, I said.

Yes yes, fine, he muttered, and hurried me into his tall, dark house.

~

Before I left Canada, Eugenio's son had said on the phone: he's happy to have you there, I promise, and you can stay as long as you like. But my dad is super socially awkward.

I didn't have a sense of what he meant until Eugenio stood in the doorway with his skittery, toothy smile swinging under the lugubrious lanterns of his eyes. The lower half of his face was joyful but from the nose up he looked as though he were sorting through the archives of the two dictatorships he had survived, laughing and in terrible pain at the same time. He moved around the kitchen in darkness, the only light coming from the blue flames of the gas stove beneath the shadowy iron skillet he used to grill meat, and the only sound from the shush of his slippers.

I strung together a couple of vapid questions.

How long have you lived in this neighbourhood? How cold does it get in winter? Eugenio made it clear that whatever he could answer would have no bearing on the success of our friendship. I don't know, twenty years and zero degrees! he stammered, then went back to slicing tomatoes and cabbage, insisting there was nothing I could do to help except set the table.

Our meal of steak, salad, and half a bottle of wine – the same meal we would have every evening I was home – was lit by the day's economic events on TV. It seemed that Argentina was always in some sort of financial crisis. I knew about the crash of the peso in 2001, when, after years of dubious fiscal management, runaway inflation destroyed the national currency. A run on banks undercut a weak system of loans. People lost life savings, retirement plans, and the value of their homes overnight. From Canada, it was referred to as "the crash," as though it were one short, sharp impact that brought the economy to the ground, a violent noise and then silence. But in Argentina it was *La Crisis*, which had an entirely different meaning. A crisis was a state of being. It was dynamic. It went on until something changed. People struggled in crisis, they struggled through it. Crisis was not a permanent state of affairs. At least semantically, a "permanent crisis" was an oxymoron, for a crisis was in relation to other possibilities. It was in contrast to a better way of being. While a crash was narrow and acute, a crisis had hope for, or at least memory of, how things could be different. A crisis included time. The Crash, *La Crisis* – it was an experience whose meaning was inflected by the words used to describe it.

Eugenio squinted at the TV with his chin up as if he were trying to see over a hill. I couldn't tell if he wanted to talk or if he preferred silence. I gambled and asked about the newspaper he edited, a weekly Communist paper called *Hoy*, which came out across the country once a week. His focus came untethered from the screen as he got up from the table and darted around in the dark to bring me the latest issue. We finished the wine and ate mandarin oranges while we talked about his master's degree in economics, his pseudonym during the last dictatorship, his family's flight to Brazil during the worst of it, the controversies and the endorsements of the books he had written, and the quality of beef in the province where he grew up. Now, at seventy-two years of age, Eugenio built his days around the weekly publication of the newspaper, collecting articles, writing e-mails, and on Tuesdays meeting with a few dedicated colleagues to do the layout before it was printed and distributed on Wednesdays. As far as I could tell, he ate steak and salad and drank a cup of wine for lunch and dinner every day, and in the mornings he drank *mate*.

I stopped drinking water years ago, he said with a nervous and endearing grin.

Then suddenly his face furrowed in concentration as though he were trying to decipher how I had appeared in his kitchen.

~

The next morning I set out for a walk in the city of my dreams, feeling both more confident and more afraid than I expected. Confident because of the haunting familiarity of a place I knew without knowing it, having read about it and absorbed it not even through the words themselves but through the spaces between the words, through the hope that surrounded the stories. Confident because my imagination had been there already and only my memory had to catch up, so that walking wasn't just discovery but confirmation, tracing a path laid by a spool of anticipated possibilities. Of course, this was what the cafés looked like. Of course, the air smelled this way.

But afraid, too, because I was now embodied and moving through those dreams. I was no longer casting my imagination beyond myself from a distant country, coming and going as I pleased, as easily as a thought. I was walking on this very street, next to real people with whom a life was possible. I was actually here. Things could happen. They could go terribly wrong.

Suddenly my plan seemed audacious, even ridiculous. What was I thinking? That I would simply arrive in a city of three million people, twelve million if you counted the suburbs, and meet writers who were willing to talk to me? How was I supposed to find them – on the sidewalk? In the grocery store? My mantra was a whisper next to the boisterous urban cacophony. The project was doomed before it had started.

I left the neighbourhood of Constitución and entered San Telmo, studying people for clues about how to belong – men with their heads down, women striding in tall shoes, old people aching with dignity. I watched a pair of hands take turns tugging at the fingertips of leather gloves, and later, a hand stirring a cup of coffee with a tiny spoon. At least I could do that.

It was after crossing Avenida Independencia, as I was walking up Defensa Street, that I felt it before I saw it. Something on the sidewalk blurred, trembling with an electric pulse that prevented me from making sense of it until the first second of shock had passed. It was a figure walking toward me. I recognized her not so much for her appearance as for the way she moved, shifts of gravity that I knew from the back of my mind. The woman lifted her head, stopped in her tracks, and opened her mouth in a mirror of my disbelief.

¿Adrián? Pero … ¿cómo? But how?

By chance, within the first hour of my first walk in Buenos Aires, I had run into a dear old friend.

Gloria was studying documentary filmmaking at the Universidad del Cine in Buenos Aires – when the program finished she would go home to Nicaragua and begin working on a project she had talked about since we were teenagers, the story of her family during the Sandinista Revolution. At the moment, she was on her way to class and didn't have much time.

I'm meeting some friends for dinner at eleven, she said, you should join us.

For the rest of the day I wandered in a cloud of bliss, thrilled to have plans so soon. The streets of Buenos Aires were built on a grid, but somehow it was the most mysterious grid I had ever explored, as though designed for getting lost. Paul Theroux (1941–) had written that it was "a wonderful city for walking, and walking I decided it would be a pleasant city to live in."[1] Another American, the poet and translator Willis Barnstone (1927–), wrote that it was "a city of walkers … whether at four in the afternoon or four in the predawn dimness, there is hardly a deserted street in this capital, and cafes and kiosks are open to serve the pedestrian."[2] I had joined the parade of foreigners from Charles Darwin to Justin Bieber who didn't hesitate to comment on the city. And, like many of them, I was enchanted by its sadness, to the chagrin of some of its inhabitants, fictional or otherwise. In the city's defence, beloved Argentine writer Leopoldo Marechal (1900–1970) had his character Adán Buenosayres remark in the 1948 novel of the same name that "it is time that *porteños* abandon their stupid reserve. The thirty-two foreign philosophers who have dishonoured us with their visits, after taking the pulse of Buenos Aires by plunging a thermometer in its anal orifice, diagnosing that our city is sad … these gringos forget that Buenos Aires is an archipelago of island-men unable to communicate with each other."[3] But it wasn't only foreigners who felt the sombre gravity of its streets. The Argentine poet Alfonsina Storni (1892–1938), who committed suicide after struggling against the machismo of the literati, wrote in her poem "Lines to the sadness of Buenos Aires": "Streets that are sad, grey, straight and equal / where sometimes you can catch a patch of sky / its dark facade and tarred ground / stifled my tepid spring dreams."[4]

There was violence in the melancholy, making it all the more urgent, intense, and visceral. Aged buildings, sturdy headstones in the cemeteries, the lines in the faces of the elderly, were made vital by the exuberance of youth striding among them. I was deliriously content to be this close to sorrow. It was a kind of truth.

Dinner that night was steak, wine, and laughter. At the table, I tried to explain to Gloria and her friends what I was doing in Buenos Aires.

What does creativity mean? I began.

Um, "creativity," someone said in English.

It sounded as if I was looking for a basic translation of the word, a one-to-one equivalent. I went on in Spanish.

Yes, but how do you understand the expectation of what it means to be creative? How would you know if something creative has been achieved?

Making something, said someone else, sawing into their steak.

Making something new, added another.

I was struck dumb. Maybe it really was that simple. The question that had brought me halfway around the world could be resolved as plainly as that. To determine if I was a creative person, all I had to do was assess whether or not I was making something new. How had I thought there was more?

But new to whom? There was historical creativity, coming up with an idea that no one else had thought of before, and there was psychological creativity, coming up with an idea that the individual hadn't thought of before, even if others had considered it – surely that was creative, too. There was a difference between big-C Creativity, so-called creative geniuses like da Vinci and Mozart who possessed "eminent creativity marked by distinguished achievements," and small-c creativity, like the baker who invented a cookie recipe based on ingredients they happened to have in the cupboard, "everyday creativity, conceived as a personal trait."⁵ Novelty and quality seemed like important aspects of a creative act, but those were hard to evaluate, too. Rolling over in bed, even if no one in all of history had rolled over in bed in that precise way before, might be novel but it wasn't significant. Or was it? In the context of modern dance, maybe it *was* creative; in terms of scientific creativity, not so much. Creativity, then, depended on what was going on around it, in relation to a socio-cultural environment. Did that mean creativity wasn't a personal attribute at all, but a social one? That it wasn't a quality, but a system? Simply making something new was not enough.

There must be more, I said.

Of course, said another of Gloria's friends. It means something different for each person who uses it, like all words.

Like all words, yes, but people keep converging on this word, creativity, as though it means something specific. I want to know what they think that is.

Picture this, I went on. Let's say two people have the flu. They are fighting it, they really want to beat it. These are combat metaphors. They describe a relationship with illness. Each one positions the patient as a soldier in battle with an adversary. In this model, they can win or lose. They are faced with a binary fate.

Maybe one of them prefers it that way: she is going to kick the shit out of the flu, and she tackles each symptom with aplomb. The thought gives her agency, power, focus. She uses it. But the other person is not a fighter. That doesn't mean he's weak, just that he feels alienated by the language of battle. He has never wanted to crush or destroy anything in his life. Plus, if the illness continues or worsens, it implies that the failure is his: he hasn't beaten it. He says he's fighting it because that's convenient. But is it the phrase that gives him the most possibility, the greatest chance to speak in harmony with his experience?

What does this have to do with creativity? said Gloria.

How we talk about our lives affects how we live. And vice versa. Language matters.

Well, it seems you've completed your research, said one of Gloria's friends, his face an implacable wall of sincerity.

To understand what people mean when they talk about creativity, I want to look at the metaphors they use, I said. I think of it as a kind of literacy – reading the personal and social significance of a concept by its metaphors in conversation. We speak in metaphors all the time. They tell us clues about how we see our reality. If we could learn to reflect on those metaphors and ask ourselves, is this the one I want? then maybe we could reinscribe our experience. We could leave our invisible, sonic mark on the history of language and offer up the unique and transient poetry of our daily lives.

Done, said the friend, either about his steak or the topic.

Very well, said someone else with the same ambiguity.

I pretended they had asked me how. I was ready with my mantra.

I want to meet writers. I want to talk to writers about writing.

Nothing happened. Cutlery clinked. Voices chattered from the tables around us.

I retreated into more questions, but I was suddenly skittish.

Can a creative experience be mapped? I squeaked. Is there such a thing as a creative process?

At that point, I became an idiot. I couldn't stop talking. It was as though the words were talking through me. I put down my fork.

Creativity is many things at once, I prattled. That's why metaphor matters. Because it makes room for multiple meanings. Each one presents new insights, layers, perspectives. Maybe it's an algorithm or a regression to childhood or a process of incubation. Maybe it's all those things, maybe it's more.

It's a little dry, no? someone chewed.

We hold different ideas about the same moment in our minds all the time, I said. And metaphor is great for representing the complexity of cognitive dissonance. It *relies* on cognitive dissonance. The whole foundation of metaphor is built on a premise that's logically incoherent. Think about it: metaphor lets me say A = B. Where's the truth in that? Yet I say it and get away with it. When it comes to understanding a concept like creativity, we need metaphor because creativity can't be pinned down to just one thing. That would contradict creativity itself!

By now I was hysterical.

Pardon? someone said, gulping wine.

It's a little dry, the friend repeated.

Are you looking at simile, too? said Gloria.

Yes, although less. Semantically they're different but cognitively they work in similar ways. Simile and metaphor expand understanding and complexity through analogous thinking. They use the concrete familiar to make sense of the abstract unfamiliar. Metaphor does it more poetically, almost magically, but simile does it, too.

And metonymy? Synecdoche?

Good point. Again, they rely on the same imaginative capacity, the ability to see one thing as another, to learn sideways, if you like. I'm using metaphors because of their ubiquity, because one can learn how to spot them like certain birds, examining their habitat. Each of those tropes – metaphor, simile, metonymy, synecdoche – draws identities together for insight. Metaphor is my point of entry into how that happens.

What a pity, no more wine, said the friend.

I rallied for my finish.

We need this kind of metaphor literacy now more than ever. It expands understanding instead of narrowing it. Everyone has access to this generative way of knowing, every time we open our mouths to speak.

It wasn't as punchy as I had hoped. I raised my fork for emphasis. My hand was sweaty and the fork slipped, clattering down the leg of my chair. When I came up from retrieving it, my face was red and the waiter was asking if we wanted anything else or could he bring the bill. Gloria and her friends nodded that the bill would be fine.

On the way out of the restaurant, one of Gloria's friends came over. Her name was Mercedes.

Why didn't you just say that you wanted to meet writers? she said. I go to a weekly seminar on contemporary Argentine literature every Saturday morning. They are young writers themselves. You'd be welcome. It's that simple.

~

I stayed up late that night, reading, trying to find my way through the thicket of metaphors that were tangled around the ambiguous meaning of creativity. The earliest metaphor I found was from the ancient Greeks. In classic mythology, creativity was the work of the muses, nine of them, who each presided over a different domain of art or science.[6] There was a muse for poetry, dance, astronomy, history, and so on. The muses were the daughters of Zeus, and their work was to breathe the stuff of life into the hearts and minds of mortals, creative life, so that when someone said he or she had "been inspired," it meant just that – they had inhaled ideas from the muses, new ways of seeing the world, which could then be expressed in works of art.[7] Those ideas were gifts, which mortals could only humbly accept. It implied that creativity didn't belong to people at all, even though it was their hands that mixed the paints and their voices that sang the songs. It certainly wasn't something that could be controlled. To be creative in ancient Greece was to submit to a muse, to a daughter of Zeus, and to have one's thoughts inhabited by hers.

Plato hadn't liked that kind of intoxication. To be taken by a muse was to embrace the irrational, and chaos with it. He believed that divine inspiration was a form of madness. It laid the conceptual foundation for his claim that poets should be banished from the republic because their work was only an imitation of reality, a form, and not an ideal.[8]

Enter Aristotle, who thought that creativity was a virtue, and virtuous behaviour was motivated intrinsically, not instrumentally.[9] But when he described an artist's work, he let slip a telling verb. The "instinct of imitation" that was so upsetting for Plato was, according to Aristotle, "implanted,"[10] a metaphor suggesting that creativity was displaced, lying somewhere outside of the human vessel, at least in its origin.

~

I had two months in Buenos Aires to find and interview the writers who would help me understand the meaning of creativity. I set about implementing the closest thing I had to a plan, making a scavenger hunt of bookstores, publishing houses, literary lectures, and salons, and contacting friends of friends with e-mails and phone calls. Then I walked.

It was during those early days that I made the transition from Adrian to Adrián. Not only did I feel different as the latter, but I could not be the former in Buenos Aires. Adrian became someone else. Hearing that name irritated me, the proof of not belonging. It mattered because words were all I was: there would be almost no pictures of me during those two months, beyond the single photo I took with each of the writers I met. I was not an image. I was barely a body. I was pure sound. It was words, starting with the name Adrián, that carried me through the city, making the city possible.

For me, living in Spanish was like living in a tent. The tent was my only home and I knew it well, how to cook, eat, clean, even make friends, but it was by nature simpler than living in a house, simpler than living in English. Things were fewer, actions were more basic. I was bolder, closer to the earth, and, in my directness, closer to honesty. It brought relief, but also fear. What happened to the complexity I had built in English, the complexity of thoughts I could no longer have? In their place, in my heart, was a fog. The tent was pitched in the margins of my inner life. Maybe I was more comfortable as Adrián because there was so much unresolved in Adrian.

Saturday morning arrived like a gust of wind. I was late. Mercedes had already texted twice to see if I was close, then a third time to say it was too cold and she had given up waiting outdoors for me.

I'll meet you inside, she said.

Facing the doorbell, I was torn between the courage to apologize and the cowardice of running away, not going to the seminar at all, when Alejandro appeared. He was one of the instructors, and also late. With a thin, high voice that seemed to be holding a ghost inside his lungs, he said that Mercedes had explained my project, that he hoped he could help, and that I was welcome to interview anyone I liked. Without being religious, I had the feeling of being blessed. In *La Gran Aldea*, the great village, one of the first texts written about Buenos Aires, Lucio V. López had written: "In Buenos Aires we are so friendly that it's easier for a foreigner who has just arrived to have the doors opened to high society, no matter who he is, than for a son of this country who has never travelled abroad."[11] Even though it had been written in 1882, it held true 130 years later.

Our footsteps echoed on the old marble as we climbed the three flights of stairs, a variation on the pilgrimage I had made to the Tower of Books in Havana. We arrived in a tall room marked by frosted glass doors. Six people, including Mercedes, were huddled around a wooden table facing a young bearded man with a tiny forehead who was drawing a line in erasable marker across a whiteboard. I nodded my apology, begging forgiveness to the group for being late, a phrase that was more accessible in Spanish than in English, conveying all of the dignity I would wish of it without sounding baroque. Alejandro, now seated, smiled with his hands folded in his lap, still wearing his jacket, while Vicente, the other instructor, waved away my apology before resuming his timeline of significant Argentine publication events at the end of the twentieth century.

The period from 1976 to 1983 had many names: *la Guerra Sucia* (the Dirty War), *el Proceso* (the Process, short for *el Proceso de Reorganization Nacional*, the Process of National Reorganization), or, more colloquially, just *la última dictadura*, the last dictatorship, because there had been several. During those years, a military dictatorship mobilized right-wing death squads to target not just anti-government guerrillas but also non-violent intellectuals, artists, professors, and workers whose activities or inclinations leaned even mildly left. As many as 30,000 people were "disappeared" – kidnapped, tortured, and killed in state detention centres and disposed of without a trace. A generation had come of age in that climate of fear and violence. Writers had found ways to keep working clandestinely, been rounded up, or fled.

The inadequate portable heater, the cold wood of the benches, and the air that was almost chilled enough to show my breath only added to the sincerity of being there. The topic itself meant less than the simple fact that we had come out for it. I learned later that Vicente and Alejandro had been instructors at the Faculty of Philosophy and Letters at the University of Buenos Aires. Their positions had since changed or ended – I didn't ask, but either one was common – and they had started this weekly seminar on contemporary Argentine literature. The group of students followed them, ranging in number from five to fifteen depending on the day and the time of year. There were readings, but no assignments. The fact that we met on a Saturday for no institutional credit, paying a small tuition to buy coffee and pastries, help the teachers, and contribute to the room, was evidence enough that what was offered had its own intrinsic reward.

Adrián, do you follow or am I talking too fast? Vicente cut into my thoughts.

I had wanted nothing more than to blend in, to be invisible, but to my disappointment he had singled me out. Until then I was only a mind, listening. The question landed in my body, making my hands sweat and my neck tingle. My thoughts scattered and regrouped. I had the feeling of hovering over the bench. An idea took shape and rolled ahead of my mind to re-form at the fingertips of my understanding. I brushed it and it rolled again to take new shapes, the shape of language in the making. No one seemed to notice the peculiar contours of my voice, yet I was shocked to be in the room, in the conversation, in the ephemera of borrowed ideas. Too soon the hour would dissolve and we would be standing on the sidewalk, saying goodbye, saying see you next week, and I would be alone again in the city, but for now I was nowhere else.

I understand, I said.

~

It was comforting to think that creativity was an exhalation from the gods. It meant that it wasn't up to me: being creative was a matter of submission. I had to be ready, to train, to practise, and to attend to inspiration when it came. In the meantime, I could get on with life. Enough with the melodramatic angst of the Artiste.

But in the intervening millennia Greek muses had fallen out of fashion and were harder to come by. They were replaced by demons or angels, biblical surrogates for the ancients.[12] The angel, like the Greek muse, was descended from the divine to animate the mortal maker from outside his or her being. It was a *conduit* metaphor for creativity, a subset of *possession*, whereby the creative person was a vessel for divine action.[13] Mozart, for example, claimed to take dictation from God while scribbling melodies in bed.[14] In a rare explanation of his creative process, Mozart wrote that he "received" his ideas in their completed form and merely had to jot them down. The drafts of his manuscripts corroborated that purity – they showed hardly any revisions.[15]

The artist's receptiveness to the angel (the Greek word *angelos* literally meant "messenger") wasn't easy to maintain. Since art came from the angel, the artist had to work hard to keep it close. That struggle, "wrestling with the angel,"[16] was a critical part of being creative, which happened only for fleeting moments of reverie before the artist was cast back into the mortal abyss. It made me think of another metaphor, the same one I had used when I was trying to explain my project to Gloria's friends: combat. The creative person had to grapple with inspiration. Losing meant being abandoned by the angel and being left to the mundane.

The benevolence of the angel was pleasant, but it didn't match what I felt were the darker undertones of creative artistic work. Something wilder, more dangerous, was at its heart. Nowhere was that demon described more eloquently than in the essay "Juego y teoría del duende" (Theory and play of the *duende*) by Spanish poet and playwright Federico García Lorca (1898–1936). The origin of the word *duende* might have been derived from "*duen de casa*," or "lord of the house,"[17] hinting again at a possession metaphor. But the *duende* was more ephemeral than a lord: it was "a force, not a labour, a struggle not a thought"[18] that gave rise to the most raw and authentic form of artistic creation. The power of the *duende* came from inside, "from the soles of the feet,"[19] and manifested itself most readily in performance – dance, song, theatre – where the artist was consumed by "dark sounds," by the haunting spectre of death that animated life. The struggle with the *duende* was more personal, more intimate, than the struggle with the angel. For, while the angel animated the creative process from outside-in, the *duende* worked from inside-out. It teased the limits of mortality, pushing into the dark force beyond life. It brought the artist to another desperate struggle: trying to achieve the impossible –

unity, purity, immortality – as a way of expressing anxiety about the world as it was given, transcending the self by engaging one's inner darkness. There was something destructive in the creative process, the possibility of "a technique to go beyond technique, [one that] ruptures the geometry of [its] own imposing forms."[20] Later, one of the writers I would interview would describe this as a central challenge in writing, how each work had to make its own rules and each subsequent work had to start again, resisting the imposing forms of habit. Creativity was an invitation to the rapture of struggling with death itself. Because the stakes were so high, the struggle wasn't just ridden with anxiety. It was violent.

I thought of a scene in *The Writing Life* by American author Annie Dillard (1945–), which described a morning that at first seemed like any other, until Dillard's typewriter began a cacophonous chatter while she was away in another room. The machine took on a life of its own, clacking and churning. Keys slammed and pages flew off the roll like a leaf storm. The seizure calmed when Dillard reached the typewriter.

"Now I know it can happen," she concluded.[21]

That was the wild abandon of the possession metaphor for creativity. The work seemed to come from somewhere else. The author wasn't even in the room. Whether it was an exploding typewriter or a struggle with an angel or a demon, the source was disassociated from the artist. To be creative meant attending to inspiration, waiting for it, responding to it, and respecting it. More than that, it meant surrender.

But was it accurate? The problem with accounts of divine intervention and possession was that they usually came from lyrical first-person confessions by artists, like Mozart or Lorca or Dillard. That didn't discredit them, but it didn't necessarily make them true either. From a scientific perspective, those testimonials were fallible. There was no way to know if they really reflected the experience they evoked, or if they were generated for some other performative purpose. And, even if they were sincere, the artist's memories were an imperfect means. People forgot how they did things, or they misremembered them. It wasn't known, for example, if Mozart was really the one to say that he "received" his notations from God. Those words might have been attributed to him by someone else.[22] All that was certain was the fluidity of the music that survived.

~

For each class there was a novel to read and each novel had to be found somewhere in the city.

The first book on the list had not been reprinted since it was published thirty years ago. I looked for it at used bookstores on Avenida Corrientes, hoping to find it without asking, since saying it out loud would betray the belonging I could maintain only in silence. It was not just that I didn't want anyone to know I was foreign but that I didn't want to know it either. As long as I scanned the shelves, tilting my head to read a title or pulling something down to leaf through it, I was the same as anyone else in the store. But when I spoke, even if what I said was clear and true and proper, my voice trembled with uncertainty. I was afraid not that I would speak incorrectly but that I was blind to particularities I could not see – that speaking right was actually wrong. After all, language had its life in the people who spoke it, and I had been in Buenos Aires only a few days.

My search of the first shop came up empty. I would have to betray myself; I would have to ask. I waited for a space to clear around the shop owner's desk. A grey-haired man with a drooping nose was leaning with his elbow on the counter, tilting his head to the side to say something to the shop owner while they both looked out at the sidewalk where the sound of umbrellas raked along a low-hanging branch near the doorway. I walked circles around the table of books as though I were unwinding a giant spool, looking down at its centre where names and words took shape. On each pass I reserved part of my vision for the man at the counter, hoping he would leave so a space would widen where I could speak to the owner.

I pulled a book from the table and flipped through it for its ink and paper. For a second I imagined the city of Buenos Aires as a dot on a high aerial map, one that was drawn on other trips to South America when I had held books in other countries. The moments when I had noticed where each one was published condensed like an accordion puffing sound onto the words, *Publicado en Buenos Aires*. I fell into that map in my mind, the dot growing larger and larger, until I was standing in the bookshop on Corrientes holding a book that was published in this very city, the heart of publishing for a continent of language.

A woman approached the counter and asked for something by Walter Benjamin. The owner nodded and pointed to the far side of the room. I practised the way she had spoken, putting my book in the place of Benjamin's and trying to match her intonation.

The man with the drooping nose showed no sign of moving from the counter. It seemed he would be there all day. I steeled myself and declared as casually as I could the title of the novel on my list. He swivelled to watch this peculiar voice. I felt him blink.

We don't have it, the owner shrugged.

My relief that the conversation was over was cut short by the disappointment that I would have to have ask at the next shop, again and again until I found the book.

I practised my query under my breath as I walked, repeating the words with my tongue moving inside my still lips, not wanting to appear crazy, wanting above all to appear familiar. This time I went straight to the counter instead of stalling at the shelves or hovering over a table, carried by the momentum of the street until the words tumbled out when I faced the shopkeeper. I thought of a cricket pitcher winding up, trotting before the throw. The sentence was my ball.

At last, success. The glue in the copy I found had dried in the thirty years since it was published and the yellowed pages fell apart like a deck of cards. I wrapped it in an elastic band, pleased that it had been so destroyed by time and use. The decay was proof of travel, connecting me to readers I had never met. Or maybe it was only a sign of the heat in a season I wouldn't know. After all, this was winter.

I read the book hunched over in cafés or cross-legged in bed, ploughing the words across the pages. My commitment was more to the act of reading as an homage to literature itself than to the book I was holding. I wanted to be inside the language of the story, to hear meaning and experience come through me by way of the book, but I didn't get much out of it. Even when the words made sense there was always a larger picture I couldn't see. I was reading, sometimes even with the twitch of a smile at certain phrases, without understanding. I had its parts but not its whole – still a genre of understanding, but I wanted more. The book was a friend who had snubbed me. I felt rejected and bitter. If it wouldn't make room for me, then I wouldn't make room for it.

I was not the kind of reader who moved across the territory of new sentences with a dictionary in hand. I paused when I came to a word I didn't know but it was a rolling stop, like coasting through an intersection at four o'clock in the morning when no one was around, a gesture of effort, a chance to look left and right before proceeding without giving up much momentum. After all, I believed in the pleasure of books. If I didn't enjoy reading, I was doing it wrong. Sometimes nothing was more pleasing than the shapes of the letters and the words. In those moments, writing was a visual object, the text a particular wall of scaffolding up the height of the page. Other times it was in a way of speaking that I heard echoing in a word or a sentence, the writing bringing a voice to life or a voice bringing the writing to life – either way I was pleased. If there was nothing in the writing, then I looked for pleasure in the act of reading itself, in the stillness and the inward gaze and in the sincerity it projected. A young man reading a novel in the window of a café made the world a better place. Even when no one saw me, when I was reading alone in bed late at night, the later the better, I believed that the city was improved by my act. Reading was a gesture of strength, of gentle self-reliance. It was evidence that one could be alone without being lonely. Whenever I saw someone reading I was relieved to know that their thoughts were somewhere else, out of reach, that they were exhibiting a wild, quiet freedom.

I had barely finished half of the first novel when it was time to discuss it in the seminar a week later. With my heart racing and my fingers numb from nervousness, I ventured a comment that began with a sentence I had copied out earlier. I cited the page number and was embarrassed by the sound of rustling as other people travelled through their books to find it. The room listened. My voice occupied the silence, a silence that had widened precisely because of my voice, making a space and filling it at the same time.

Si, buena lectura, Vicente said, good reading, and continued my comment in his own words. He added a detail to his timeline on the board and flipped the marker in the air while he talked. I exhaled into a room that I had joined, as if the conversation were a heavy truck hurtling past and I had moved close enough to be pulled along by the wind that travelled with it.

The next novel was still in print. I found it at El Ateneo, one of the most glorious and spectacular bookstores in the world. The store had been converted from an opera house. The main floor, the balconies, and the box seats were filled with books and what once was the stage was now a café hung with long velvet curtains. I understood little of the second book's tone, except for a few descriptions of swamps and disease that thrilled me because of how vividly they appeared, but when it came time for the class I realized that I hadn't understood much of its plot, either, since I had invented an entirely different story than the one we talked about. From our conversation I learned that the author was being ironic in his socio-literary critique. I already knew that irony and comedy were the last sensibilities one learned in a language that wasn't one's own. Instead, though, I found my pleasure in the abundance of natural nouns that cropped up in the book. Every paragraph was full of birds, trees, and grass, things I couldn't get much of in the city. These nouns, true to their linguistic category, were objects in my mind, things I clung to as I moved through the abstraction of the sentence. I held on to them. The more objects, the easier it was to stay up. Verbs, too, kept me afloat. Together they carried me on the surface of the story without sinking.

But story, at best, was all I got. Only rarely did I feel the work's poetry, the rush of air that lifted me clean beyond the things and the doing into another way of being with language, a way of being beyond language, delivered by a turn of phrase. In those moments, the words smiled through me, language finding my face as text and expression mixed. Then the text moved away and I was only looking at it again.

The other books I found in smaller shops in the chic neighbourhood of Palermo: Librería Lilith, where a friend knew the owner; Eterna Cadencia, where I would have my second interview; and Crack-up, named, I assumed, after the essay by F. Scott Fitzgerald. When I found a shop I liked, I dreamed up excuses to go back the next day or the day after. The books in Buenos Aires were slender and discrete, bearing smooth, matte covers, substantial paper, confident ink, produced by houses of every size. Their appearance was modest, which gave them dignity, and none flashed hyperbolic endorsements the way they did in Canada. They were not advertisements, they were books, and because they were "just" books they penetrated deep into the aura of what a book could be – archetypal, simple enough in design to be universal. With the reading list for the seminar and the titles of works by the writers I hoped to meet, I had good reason to find, open, hold, touch, smell, and even read many books all over the city. Those peaceful routines could have kept me happy for a long time.

Then one evening I was walking home along Avenida Santa Fe. It was late. I crossed the street and stepped onto the sidewalk just in time to feel the city freeze. It lasted less than a second. Two boys on a motorcycle tore through the dark, riding fast against the traffic, racing down the aisle between the cars. Blue lights and screaming sirens came after them on two other motorcycles. Cars swerved. Horns wailed. The boy on the back of the motorcycle held tight to the driver, his skinny arms wrapped around the latter's chest, his white T-shirt chattering in the wind like a crazy flag. Then they were gone.

When the traffic resumed, the city was not the same. Something had been revealed: violence, flight, the chase. I walked back to Constitución aching with what I knew. A pursuit like that could end only when one of them made a mistake, turned too fast, risked too much, outdid himself to outdo the other, and either the boys or the police would sail over the traffic to lay broken on the street – all for a purse or a wallet. For that one moment, the driver of the boys' motorcycle had been alive and terribly free while his friend clung to him, wishing he could get down, time out, it's too much, I can't do this anymore. I thought of their mothers, the mothers of the boys and the mothers of the police, in separate worlds that never met except through their sons on a night like this, and the news that would bring one of them to the floor in the doorway of her apartment. In my mind, the motorcycles circled the city all night, that split second repeating on every street until hours had gone by and nothing had changed, everyone was still racing into the future, so that in the morning when I heard sirens pass by the house I was sure it must be them.

~

For the scientist who was dissatisfied with lyrical testimonials, there was the metaphor *creativity is evolution*. It drew on a Darwinian vision of traits and selection as they operated in species and directed it at understanding the creative process in individuals.[23] In the biological application of Darwin's theory of evolution, species diversified through the blind process of mutation. Traits that improved a species' survival were selected for continuation, with the organism that exhibited those traits passing them on to its next of kin when it reproduced. Applied to creativity, the evolution metaphor entailed two stages that reflected biological stages: (1) the blind generation of ideas, and (2) the selection of the best fit, depending on the needs of the project.[24] It meant that people who were more productive – people who had more ideas – would have a higher rate of success. They would be better able to select an idea for its best fit to their creative work.[25] To make that selection, they had to see relationships. They had to see connections that others couldn't, finding generative remote associates.[26] It was a process of juxtaposing the familiar with the unfamiliar. The more remote the associates were, the more original the combination tended to be.[27] The ability to access diverse ideas was the foundation of creative potential because having diverse knowledge meant greater chances for unique pairings.

It wasn't a perfect theory. First, it put a strong emphasis on the role of chance.[28] Sure, chance was important in creative work,[29] but there were other factors, too, like the commitment to developing an idea in spite of resistance. Simply generating more ideas didn't necessarily lead to a creative outcome if none of the ideas were any good, or if none of them were sufficiently developed.

Second, ideas were not universally viewed as separate entities that lay dormant, waiting to be selected for elaboration or "fit" with a larger project.[30] In other words, not all understandings of creativity saw ideas as disparate but combinable units. This would become more apparent as my catalogue of metaphors grew.

Finally, maybe the evolution metaphor just didn't translate from one domain to the other. Maybe the biological model for how change accumulated applied to living organisms without applying to the generation of creative ideas. In biology, a seal that lost a fin in a battle with an orca whale didn't give birth to finless offspring, yet once someone had the idea to attach a handle to a door, doors with handles were widely adopted.[31] Creative change accumulated differently than biological change. And yet one could still convey meaning by saying that an idea had "evolved," meaning that it was no longer the same as the way it started, that it had passed through different stages of growth.

~

In the year before I went to Buenos Aires, I took tango classes in Vancouver – something to get me out of the house, something to teach me how to lead. My instructor spent half the year in Buenos Aires. Since I was leaving Canadian summer for Argentine winter, effectively travelling backwards against the seasonal trend, she was north when I was south. I offered to deliver a small package to a friend on her behalf, the pretext for an introduction.

On a grey winter's day in June, I met Silvia for *medialunas* – half-moons, croissants – at a café near her apartment in San Telmo. She talked about taking care of her mother and about her son, who had moved away with his family, and described an institute where I could take drawing classes if I wanted, la Asociación Estímulo de Bellas Artes, the Association for Encouraging the Arts. We finished our coffees and walked slowly through Plaza Dorrego where she pointed out art she didn't like, shrugging with her palms upward in the air, rolling her eyes and saying, but what do I know?

We got along well, and met again the following Sunday to visit an art gallery in La Boca. We walked there slowly from Silvia's apartment, talking about art and love, and about how one's parents were inevitably one's model of what a relationship looked like. Silvia asked if my parents were still together and I said yes, and that each time I saw them they seemed to be more in love, or that love was always becoming something new.

Que lindo, que bueno, she said wistfully.

I wondered if I would ever find that kind of longevity or if my relationships would always be measured in months or in a couple of years or if I might even give up on the idea entirely, defeated. She asked if that was the case. I told her I had just broken up with someone after two years together.

Did you live together?

Yes.

How was it?

Sometimes it was really good.

Did you speak the same language?

I thought we did. But I looked inward to find myself and she looked outward.

That's another language, said Silvia.

It was like trying to build a bridge between two distant shores, I said. The thrill came from knowing that I could find myself on the other side, but then I couldn't do it anymore because I hadn't figured out how to recover, how to keep building the bridge and eventually it, or I, or we, collapsed.

Silvia paused for a moment before replying.

It's good that your relationships are like that, she said, a few months or even a few years. At your age they are supposed to be that way and it's good that you're moving around, coming to know yourself. It's too much to get tied down too early, especially when your heart is open. I can see that you're searching for yourself and I think you should keep searching.

We reached the port and walked beside the brown water of the Rio de la Plata to the Museo de Bellas Artes de Benito Quinquela Martín, the restored house of an autodidactic painter who had found success ninety years before, painting the lives of the men who unloaded the ships – the fires, the iron, the barrels they carried. Silvia and I wandered among the big work, nodding at the way he rendered the reflection of the sky and the red in the fires using fat brushes and thick paint.

After sunset, when it wasn't safe to walk in La Boca, we took a *colectivo* back to San Telmo. We visited the same café we had been to a week before. It was more crowded this time, maybe because winter had installed itself more obviously over the city in the interval, and there was only one empty table at the back of the room. I showed Silvia some pages from my sketchbook while we waited for our coffees.

I think you should pursue this, she said, these drawings, apart from your studies. There's something here that you need to follow.

Look, she continued, two things are important for good art, at least the kind of good art we saw in the gallery. You need to be a good drawer and you need to know how to use colours.

I'm not very good with colours, I said.

Me, I am, said Silvia. I know how to stop before they get dirty.

I always dirty them, I mumbled.

Start with just two colours and work with those until you understand them together. Then little by little, begin working with three, but leave that for later.

Just two colours, I repeated.

Like what you're doing with your charcoals, she said. They're good, you can draw, you have that. I can see that you're shy about going to the drawing classes I mentioned but you should know that I'm pushing you, I'm blowing a breath of air behind you to encourage you to go through the door, even though you're reluctant to do it.

She filled her cheeks with air and blew across the table.

How had she known about my shyness regarding the art classes? Or understood my need to looked inward to find a place in the world?

I know, she said, because I'm like that, too.

~

The evolutionary metaphor hinted that creativity was an accumulation of changes over time, an advancing line of growth. But what if the very thing that made an idea creative was how it deviated from that line?

In 1950, when the president of the American Psychological Association gave his annual address, he advocated research not just on intelligence but on creativity, too.[32] According to his speech, creativity required new ways of thinking, and that meant breaking away from the past. It also meant being sensitive to problems – if someone was dissatisfied with a tool, they might try to devise a better one. If someone saw no inadequacies with a tool, they wouldn't. The implied metaphor was that *creativity is divergence*, meaning that creativity required thinking in a way that went against convention, thinking that took a different turn. It implied coming up with alternatives to the present and expanding the notion of normal. It was a conscious, methodical act of deviating from the familiar in favour of the mysterious.

But a careful balance had to be struck between diverging and simply blasting off into irrelevance. Surely creativity wasn't just about doing something different for the sake of being different. When people talked about being creative, they imbued it with some sort of value. Creativity was meaningful – not necessarily practical, for there were plenty of paintings that had yet to save a life, but it was significant in the way it participated in a historical conversation. It could not stretch too far into obscurity or it would break with that significance. Deviation from a path was in relation to the path. Otherwise it would cease to be deviation. There was a tradition, a pattern, and there was a break toward something else that mattered.

~

I could not forget one drawing from the last room of the gallery in La Boca. It was a street scene with buildings looming over a stooped figure in the bottom right side of the frame. The drawing was taller than I was. The figure's face was the same size as my face. Lines had been scratched deep beside his eyes, making him look old. He was wearing a triple-pointed crown, and his expression was comic, but tragically so, like a jester who had been banished from a kingdom that very night and now wandered the dark city, bewildered. Three other figures slunk beside him, much smaller, softened into the shadow of the walls, and each one wore the same triple-pointed crown. All of them hurried desperately deeper into the shadows. High above, on a broken bridge that spanned halfway across the street, a man was striding with long, skinny legs into the abyss of a vacant part of the page. The drawing was by an artist named Ricardo Ajler. It was called "Pordioseros."

Because it was the first time I had seen that word, its meaning was defined by the image of the charcoal men with their crowns, their demeanour that of reluctant wizards, their expression suggesting a desire to tell secrets. I repeated the word out loud as I walked home, softening the sounds with my mouth until they opened: *por*, for; *dios*, god. The for-gods? The for-god's-sake? The people-for-god?

None of those seemed to fit.

The word slid from the mystical to the impoverished, from the residents of a magical city to those who lived on a street made of dry, black powder, while part of the word still clung to dignity and asceticism. A dictionary would have said it meant simply "beggars," but that wasn't enough. They had crowns, they had a city of their own. Nothing in English matched its strange and beautiful nuance. *Pordiosero* was a point of convergence – or was it refraction? – for the drawing, the dictionary, and the etymology of the word. But it was also an ever-changing record of experience.

For to understand the concept of [beggar] – I imagined it with square brackets because it was paraphrased from the experience of what the word represented – I could look to the word "beggar" – in quotation marks because it was the word itself. But, if I wanted to understand its complexity, I could look for words that might be used in a similar moment, which was how I came to *pordiosero* and the concept of [*pordiosero*]. "Beggar" was not the same as *pordiosero*, but the two words communicated with each other since they were used in similar circumstances. If an English speaker and a Spanish speaker found themselves impoverished, one might become a beggar and the other might become a *pordiosero*. The person who could be both beggar and *pordiosero* multiplied their identity, becoming a composite, the site where different meanings met. That person brought one meaning beyond itself to another meaning. In other words, they made metaphor.

~

An *algorithm* metaphor for creativity was a more elaborate version of the divergence metaphor. It meant that the mind was a machine.

Through an algorithmic process, the theory went, one anticipated future outcomes based on cause-and-effect principles that extended from knowledge of existing conditions.[33] All processes of mind, creative or otherwise, were knowable as algorithmic processes of combination. If something so new and novel arose that was inexplicable by the model, it could be attributed only to (1) algorithms that were not yet understood, (2) chance, or (3) "dynamic chaos" – itself a semi-algorithmic theory, if an unresolved one.[34]

The mental machine that performed the algorithmic work was far from perfect. There was no single act of creation, but rather an engagement over time. It was often an "endless enslavement to inevitable difficulties rather than a single or all-resolving Eureka-like determination."[35] The model of a frustrated creative engagement ran counter to Plato's belief that the artist began with a vision of truth or beauty and tried to set that vision down to the best of his abilities[36] – and it was *his* abilities, since it was doubtful that Plato imagined female artists. Still, it was helpful to think of creativity as a mechanistic, instrumental engagement, even if that machine was prone to breakdown or mechanical failure.

The algorithmic model of creativity was comforting, for it made room for logic and reason in what otherwise was too often reduced to whimsy. Creativity was serious stuff, and nothing said "serious" like machines and algorithms. But the metaphor had its limits, as they all did. If, as Plato claimed, the artist began with a vision and tried to get that vision down as well as he could, how was one to account for the deviations that the artist took along the way toward reaching that goal, deviations that might otherwise have been considered creative except that they were not fixed to the original vision? Those shifts in treatment that arose *during* the creative process were still creative. In fact, they might have been the most creative part. If creativity was to be understood as the transformation of a vision into a thing, or, in Plato's terms, the expression of an ideal in a form, then a lot of the creative process was left out.

The algorithm metaphor for creativity assumed a causal relation between different stages of the creative engagement, but if those causal relations were limited to what was already fixed and determined by an algorithmic formula, then maybe the result wasn't that creative at all.[37] Unless, I wondered, there was a difference between creativity of means and creativity of ends. One could know the end and still be creative about how to get there.[38] But something still bothered me. There was a sticky relationship between the algorithm and divergence. Divergence could be part of an algorithm, it could be incorporated as one of the methods for creative production, but what happened when one diverged from the algorithm itself?

~

Each day, I set out for the intersection of Avenida Callao and Corrientes, believing that it was the centre of the city. And each day, upon arriving, I was forced to leave it behind, unsure how long I could stand on the corner before feeling lost, purposeless, and used up.

Some days I turned east toward the obelisk that stood distantly at Avenida 9 de Julio, moving in a straight line and then, as I felt more adventurous, taking side streets north or south while still wending my way in its direction to pop out on the avenue at different points but always with the obelisk in sight. Later, when I walked farther from the obelisk, I kept it in mind, like a pin holding the fabric of the city in place. When I was more comfortable in Buenos Aires, I avoided the centre altogether, the obelisk and the intersection of Callao and Corrientes, since they seemed too predictable, too hasty and impersonal. The life of the city that I wanted to know extended along the streets away from it.

It was the same with learning a language: at first, I searched for the biggest monuments of Spanish. I had to find the places that were the heart of its use – I had to understand the obelisks and the Corrientes. The peripheries of language, like the peripheries of the city, were a mystery. I wasn't sensitive to their nuances, their quieter spaces, and to dedicate myself to them seemed like an overly meticulous project when there were such big signals of life mixing and exchanging at the centre.

When I could predict what I would find on Avenida Corrientes before I even got there, it was time to choose the streets that led away from it – like arriving at a familiar sentence when it was time to find another way to say it. I walked west, away from the obelisk, feeling at first that I was leaving the city behind, having no idea how far it stretched. The trees overhead stooped to embrace the street and there were more second-hand bookshops, then those faded away and became boutiques, restaurants, cafés, and office buildings. Sidewalks divided around billboards and apartments. Pavement broke apart. Familiar street names were markers that I laid down in the mental map I was writing, places where what I had thought was unknown in fact crossed with something known, a street near my house that intersected with one far away – busier, peopled with a different class of fashion, or calm and empty – so that the logic of the city was safe and wild at the same time. The continuation of streets I had crossed in other parts of the city was proof that I would not get totally lost, not on a map nor in my mind, that I could find my way back as long as I knew where to find the major avenues, the key phrases, the words to get me home. All I had to do was pay attention to how I had got there and attend to what was ahead, not so I could retrace my steps, which I refused to do, but so that my map of language and city grew denser, more personal, with every foray. It was the same with my voice, for when I thought I was lost in the labyrinth of a sentence, I pressed on, sometimes blindly but always with hope, until I found something familiar in words.

By the end of my time in Buenos Aires, I went to Corrientes only when it served as a meeting place, since the intersection with Callao was an easy landmark. I was no longer drawn to the obelisk, no longer needed it to orient myself, having realized that it was a false centre to a city that was diffused all around it. At its busiest places the noise of the city masked its subtleties. Language was happening at the outskirts, where words, like streets I knew, were crossing ones I had never known before.

~

The writers I tried to contact were slow to reply, if they replied at all. What would happen if no one wanted to talk to me? Maybe I was doing it all wrong. Maybe it was best not to worry so much about the question. Maybe there was a certain limit to what I could do to develop an idea so long as it remained in conscious thought. Relax, I thought. Enjoy being here. I had sent out a dozen e-mails to writers I was connected to by a degree or two of separation. The ball was in their court. There was nothing to do but wait. Maybe it was the same with creative processes.

Ernest Hemingway claimed that he wrote each morning until the afternoon, when it was time to go and do something else, like visit the racetrack or take a long walk. It was during that time away from the writing, he believed, that the writing worked itself out so that he had something to write the next day. In his memoir *A Moveable Feast*, he reflected, "I learned not to think about anything that I was writing from the time I stopped writing until I started again the next day. That way my subconscious would be working on it and at the same time I would be listening to other people and noticing everything, I hoped; learning, I hoped; and I would read so that I would not think about my work and make myself impotent to do it."[39]

The philosopher Bertrand Russell (1872–1970) had a similar belief, claiming that if you worked hard on a creative project, or on problem solving of any nature, it was best to put it aside at some point and do something else. The problem had usually been solved by "the unknown forces that operate underground" by the time he returned to it.[40]

Hemingway and Russell implied that creativity was a process of *incubation*, the argument that creative ideas came from letting them sit in the subconscious for a while.[41] It reflected into a larger sequence of stages articulated in 1926 by the cognitive psychologist Graham Wallas (1858–1932).[42] His model had it that the creative process passed through four distinct stages: preparation, incubation, illumination, and verification. The linearity of the model had since been criticized, arguing for "fluid" stages, but the titles of each stage still emphasized their scientific origins.[43]

The implication was simple: work hard, play hard. Or if not hard, then at least oscillate between work and play, focus and distraction. Stay open to thinking that seemed unrelated to the problem at hand, for it was during those moments that other work was being done in the background of thought. I recognized this process from the times I had been commissioned for a drawing or an illustration. After I reviewed the request, ideas came on their own, during the night or during long walks. All I had to do was give them time.

~

Then, just like that, a good day ballooned to the surface without warning or trace. The space around it widened, taking on the colour of grey like the rooftops of the city at dusk, when a wild ribbon of bliss unfurled upward from one of the streets. It started with three hours of writing in a café – my first short story in Spanish, then suddenly a glimpse of my second. I was sitting in the only café in the world writing the only story there was to tell with the only pen in the only notebook. Writing had reconfigured loneliness as an intentioned intimacy, a communion with being. It was a way of loving.

When it was time to go it was time to go: I folded up my belongings without hesitation, rested and thrilled with the knowledge that I had worked that day. What mattered most was the energy of what I had written down – not the story itself, which I would care less and less about until, after weeks had passed, it embarrassed me – but the experience of moving something into the world. I walked as though every turn took me deeper into the city and into myself. Every street seemed to have been built for my discovery.

I arrived just in time to hear the last of the free music that played three times a week at the Centro Cultural San Martín. I couldn't stop smiling as I soaked in the sound. When it ended I tumbled out onto the street again, moving as if I had somewhere to go, when really all I wanted was to drift in and out of the thick crowd on Corrientes, slipping between the shoulders of strangers.

I bought drawing supplies, sticks of charcoal, and the long roll of paper that Silvia recommended. There was no better proof of belonging than walking with a long roll of paper –what tourist had such business here? It was as precious to me as a flag.

At the butcher's shop on the corner of San Juan and Entre Ríos, I bought two kilograms of beef. When I asked for the cuts that Eugenio had specified, there was a note of his voice in mine. It fortified me and made it easy to stand by the counter as the butcher traced his knife through the red meat as if he were drawing lines with a pen, the steaks leaning one on top of the other on the wax paper. I watched his thumbs, his knuckles and his fingers, their thickness, and how softly the big knife moved.

That evening I walked to San Telmo for my first tango lesson with Patricia. My teacher in Vancouver had recommended her. The class was open to anyone but because it was winter I was the only student. Patricia and I spent an hour drifting over the tiled floor of a café basement. For the length of one song, one tremendous song that I felt more than heard, as though in fact the room were totally silent and there was nothing but the brush of our footsteps to tell us what to do, we walked as one person. It was the simplest thing, just walking, but walking so much together that each time I stepped forward I was moving into air that was charged with the life of someone else.

Tango is a dance that's made with two feet, said Patricia. One foot from the man and one foot from the woman. If there are four feet, there's a problem.

For the length of a song, I understood what she meant.

I walked home, made dinner with Eugenio, and later fell asleep thinking: there is so much here to learn, which was another way to say that there is so much here to feel.

That day stayed streaming quietly upward, a plume of joy among others that in their moment were steady and grey – at least that was how they were in the moments I chose to write them down. Months later I would have the legacy of the words I found when I was there, the notes in my journal, which I would use as evidence that such ecstasy was real. How was it that some of those feelings rose so high above the stretch of time? In that moment when the goodness of the day coalesced into one decisive approval, I was infinite. Only my body contained me, and even that seemed ready to burst. The momentum by which I tumbled into Avenida Corrientes from the Centro Cultural was the same as the momentum that tumbled into me from the focused act of writing.

Back in Canada, I would be able to summon that feeling only by writing my way into it. I would revisit my notes and burrow into memory with these words. I had to trust that such a day really happened, that it really was so good. There would be no sign of it on my body, no scar or mark, no residue except the invisible trace that feelings left on existence – that day passed like a feather across the palm of my hand. I would try to celebrate in the way I wrote it, stay true to the celebration I believed in then. Each little day calibrated my larger sense of the city, just as words came together to make a language.

But it took more than words to make a language. It was the experience of those words that mattered most. A new word appeared at a distance, opaque and hard. On first encounter I could see it, notice its location, but had no idea what was inside. It was a pebble hovering in the air just out of reach. Then as I came to know it, understanding the circumstances of its utterance, it opened. It was no longer a stone. It had more in common with an exotic fruit covered in a grey peel, with red soft pulp inside, and knowing it meant turning the peel inside out.

When I thought of words as stones I saw that they were carefully arranged, mostly in lines, along a page or in the air when people spoke. When I thought of words as fruits I saw that language was the juice that came from squeezing them.

~

In an interview cited in the *Guardian* newspaper,[44] the late Steve Jobs said, "When you ask creative people how they did something, they feel a little guilty because they didn't really do it, they just saw something. It seemed obvious to them after a while." It was an *illumination* metaphor, revealing new insights into a project. Illumination could come after a certain amount of incubation had occurred or it might happen the first time someone set eyes on a problem. It suggested that people at certain moments of creative insight "can detect clearly and directly something others have to squint to see."[45] Illumination of this sort happened when all the preparation stages were resolved and a reinterpretation of knowledge was allowed, implying new relationships, the disappearance of anomalies, and seeing the project in a new light (to continue the luminous metaphor).[46] It was that cartoon moment when a bulb went on above someone's head.

Another way of understanding this view on creativity was just that – that creativity was a certain view, a perspective, and that the creative contribution was one of perceiving the challenge from a new angle.[47] That new angle might not come after staring indefinitely at the same words or the same image. Maybe the idea had to be transitioned from conscious thought to unconscious thought so it could emerge on its own into the light of creative resolution. For example, the poet Ralph Waldo Emerson (1803–1882) wrote that creativity didn't come from staying at home or from travelling but from moving between the two.[48] The epiphanic gestalt of a creative process revealed itself more readily when its mental pursuit was engaged in transitions between dark (unconscious thought, incubation) and light (conscious thought, contemplation), implying that creativity meant shifting between spatial and mental domains.

~

The instructor of my first drawing class at the Estímulo de Bellas Artes was more suited to a job in late-night radio than fine art. He spent the hour making long strings of words that he looped over my drawings in lazy circles, talking without prompt or content, and I was trapped nodding at his epic monologue, realizing that a simple question would wind him up again and even a pre-historic grunt would inspire him to adjust my drawing with what he meant, narrating every move. The glances I stole at my easel only made him talk faster and move his hands in the air with greater vigour until I forcibly turned away. He talked for a while longer before drifting to another student where he wrapped a similar spool of words around her work. Somehow she kept drawing as though he weren't there.

In spite of his droning commentary, I was triumphant as I marched into the studio, pretending that I really had the confidence to be there, taking a drawing board from where they leaned against the wall, adjusting my easel, arranging my charcoals, and facing the model that lay reclined on the cloth-covered wooden boxes in the middle of the room. I drew quickly at first, too quickly, contending with the certainty that my drawing would fail; then I passed the threshold of disaster and it seemed that my figure would be human after all. I breathed out. It was a relief to work without words.

On Silvia's encouragement, I went back for another class with shorter poses and a different teacher. The second instructor, a muralist, was a trudging, heavy man with wisps of white hair above his ears. If the other teacher could moonlight in radio, this one was meant for meditation. I watched him spend ten minutes beside another student's easel, looking only at the artist's face as though he expected to find in her expression the missing link between the life of the model and the image on the paper.

I dreaded his critique as I waited my turn. I filled the silence with every horrible thought he might have about my drawing. But when he came around to my easel I was surprised by my calm, knowing that I was somehow outside of the weak shapes I had conjured in charcoal. It might have been because it was not my language, not my city or my country, not my way of doing things, that I relaxed enough to feel the weight of my arm in my shoulder as my hand drifted over the paper and I could say to myself, *Adrián, tranquilo*, he is just a man with experience, learn from him. And so, when the teacher broke the silence by pointing at what I had drawn, asking me to look again at the curve in the model's spine, I could smile and say without shame or apology, You're right.

During the break, a woman who had shown me around the studio got into an argument with the model, who was warming up with her jacket on, drinking *mate*, and eating a cookie. Without any context that I could detect, the woman explained that everyone was entitled to the same rights, which meant that everyone should live by the same limitations, too, including the president of Argentina.

It's unjust that the president's children get to travel in a helicopter, the woman spat. If we are all equal then we're all equal.

The model, who was less than half her age, said that was ridiculous and sure, we can say we're all equal but of course the president's children are going to have privileges that we don't have.

The woman shouted back at her, saying it was wrong and unjust and what kind of country was this when even the youth wouldn't listen?

I'm listening to you, said the model, but the woman kept shouting, Listen to me, listen to me, as if they were both trying to put their hand on top of the other's hand in a tower that would never be out of the other's reach.

The rest of us kept passing *mate* and eating cookies. It was pleasant not to be the spectacle.

I'm listening but the world doesn't work like that! said the model.
Well what kind of world do you want to live in?!

The instructor shook his head and made a tisking noise, wandering between them. Back to work then? he yawned.

~

What if creativity was really about returning to a younger mind?

Freud thought that creative thinking was to be attributed to primary process thinking, which was connected to the *id* of one's personality.[49] Because primary process thinking was layered over with the secondary process thinking that was acquired through aging and experience, we might not be aware of what our *id* was thinking. Creative people were those who could continue exploring their primary process thinking long after childhood, when it typically expressed itself, and use it toward novel ways of solving problems in their adult lives.

The theory that *creativity is regression* was sometimes presented as a myth about creativity, outdated and no longer useful.[50] It continued to circulate as a metaphor even if it was no longer valuable as empirical truth. The metaphor was helpful on another level, though, for it made room for the possibility that *creativity is play*. By this metaphor, the creative act was linked to the ability to recall childhood forms of make-believe and to bring them into creative projects in adulthood. The physicist Richard P. Feynman (1918–1988), for example, insisted on starting projects again on his own so that he could render diagrams in a way that he felt was satisfying. He maintained that his method of engaging with research problems was pure play.[51]

~

At the end of one of the drawing classes, the woman who believed in equal rights and equal limitations asked where I was from.

Canada, I told her.

Do you speak English or French?

English.

She took my hand and led me across the room to a tall woman with a smile that flickered like an old film. This woman had been coming to the drawing class for months but didn't speak a word of Spanish. Could I translate for her?

When the tall woman heard that I spoke English, all the lights in the theatre of her face lit up. She hugged me and vigorously kissed my cheek. Her name was Rita. She had been living in Buenos Aires for two years, from Australia. Her husband was a tango teacher – she had danced with him one night in Sydney and "that was that." She shook her head sadly.

You must come over for dinner, she said.

I hadn't come to Buenos Aires to speak English but I was grateful for her generosity in a city where I didn't know many people. I couldn't imagine the loneliness of living for two years without the language of a place, how alienating it would be and how, inevitably, that alienation would become normal. She was both courageous and terrified, perplexed that time had passed so quickly and that she had grown smaller and smaller inside herself. Her drawings, which were superb, were the only voice she had for commenting on her surroundings. At the same time, they were a way of looking inward – willowy, faint, ethereal. It was the same with writing, I thought: looking inward to comment on the world.

Two days later I walked to her house. It was nine o'clock at night and the streets were dark. I had studied the map before leaving home, nudging my route through the city with my eyes, choosing the streets I knew by watching the names light up in my mind. With each familiar word I saw an image of the sidewalk, the street, some buildings, and a presence that shone as if from the hearts of the people who I remembered walking there, while the streets I hadn't walked stayed dark without memories to light them.

But as I made my way to Rita's house I wondered if I had looked at the map too hastily. I believed that the name of her street would slide into place as though declaring its own truth because I was looking for it, because she had said it, like the name itself was expecting me, but all I saw were buildings and shadows and trees without leaves.

I had a map in my pocket, but I didn't want to look lost. If I could be lost without anyone knowing it, then I was quite content. I took it as a sign of belonging. But to be lost and look lost was another matter, and possibly a dangerous one. I was surprised by how many places I had been in the world without being accosted, a safety I attributed to a simple practice of walking with intention and not gawking at everything I saw. But there was no more obvious a declaration of not belonging than standing on a sidewalk, looking up and down the street and then up and down another street, holding a map.

In Buenos Aires I learned to lean in doorways if I needed to check where I was, get off the sidewalk, position myself on a step, put my back to the wall, preferably not right under a street lamp where my bewilderment became a theatrical display, but off to the side so that the light fell across the page of the map. If there was another step behind me then I hitched one foot up in a way I had seen other men do. If something bad were to happen on a busy street, it was more likely to be pick-pocketing, which wasn't really that bad compared to violence. If something bad happened on an empty street, violence seemed inevitable. Why go to all the trouble of being sneaky for a little reward when you could be direct and get more? I looked around and glumly concluded that I was alone.

I tried to find the tiny blue sign that would say what street I was on. I was squinting in the dim light when I heard footsteps. Without looking back, I turned down the street to the right and walked as quickly as I could, thinking of what one of Gloria's friends had said when I was going back to Constitución late one night: If anything happens, just run. That's the only advice I can offer you.

The footsteps followed me onto the same street, echoing between the empty, lamp-lit walls. I crossed to the opposite sidewalk and strained from the corner of my eye to see my pursuer. He was about forty years old with hunched shoulders. His hands were stuffed into the pockets of his black jacket. He looked over his shoulder behind him the same way I had done.

When he crossed to my side of the street, the muscles in my legs filled with tingly light. My hands were sweating and an invisible weight pressed down on the back of my neck, above my spine, as if a beam would strike me there any minute and send me sprinting.

The footsteps stopped a few paces away. Keys jingled. A door creaked and shoes scuffed twice before the door creaked again. The street went quiet. The light from my muscles pooled in my knees and didn't go away.

Then, up ahead, something pounded against the wall and a group of quick shoes roughed the dry street. I couldn't see where it had come from because of the trees and the shadows cast by the lamps. The same sound pounded again on the wall and there was a sliding noise. Someone had fallen. A young man's voice cackled in the dark.

Shit shit shit shit shit shit, I muttered in fluent English.

I walked toward the sound.

Why toward it? At what point, I wondered, would I turn and run? Would I always wait a minute longer, a minute longer until it was too late, believing until the end in the possibility that everything would be fine? I kept walking because I hadn't stopped walking, because momentum seemed like the only thing that would get me out of where I was. Later, it would seem so simple to stop, turn around, walk back, return up the hill, or else, if I must continue, then go down a different street. But the boys had already seen me.

There were four of them, about sixteen years old, playing soccer in the empty street. The ball struck the wall of the opposite building.

Their game was focused around the other sidewalk, enough room to pass behind. I walked under alternating lamplight and tree shadows. None of the boys looked up. None of them seemed to care that I was there. I turned down the hill to whatever the city had in store.

Another man came up the hill against me. I felt my stomach tense and my shoulders relax.

He passed, breathing hard because of the incline. I crossed behind him and leaned against a wall, hitching one foot up on the step to study my map – there was no other choice. Above on the wall there was a house number and street name. I laughed.

It was Rita's house.

~

The Chilean-Argentine-American Ariel Dorfman (1942–) wrote about the complexity of home in his memoir *Heading South, Looking North: A Bilingual Journey*, reflecting, "I was consoling myself with one of the basic myths of the species, a story that every civilization has told itself since the beginning of history: there is a place, one place, where you truly belong, a place that is often but not always the place where you were born, and that place is akin to paradise."[52]

Buenos Aires was that place for me, that borrowed home, or so I believed. I belonged there even before I arrived. And after I had left, part of me would always be there, still walking, still writing, still wondering what I would become if I stayed. It reminded me that not all metaphors for creativity emphasized process. The metaphor *creativity is a place* highlighted the geographic and spatial qualities of creativity and looked at the ways that creativity was projected onto location. While the angel and the demon arose from poetic work and divergence and combination arose from cognitive psychology, the spatial attributes of the place metaphor could be considered a geographer's vision of creativity.

Shifting the research emphasis from "creative person" to "creative situation" acknowledged the important role that environment played in generating creative activity.[53] For years, the thought of Buenos Aires had conjured imagery and narratives about creative culture as I anticipated what I would find there. The same could be true for, say, New York or Paris, which drew people with dreams of inspiration just by historical reputation. On a smaller scale, it could be true of an artist residency or attending a certain school, even working from a certain room of a house. Place became a screen upon which expectations were projected, expectations of creativity or any other attribute.[54] These "priming effects" influenced how people thought and behaved there, even before arriving.[55]

The metaphor *creativity is a place* implied a larger, encompassing metaphor: *creativity is an attitude*.[56] It suggested that the spatiality of creativity arose out of a collective sense of expectation that individuals projected onto the community. The community was the agent of the metaphor, the host of the projections cast upon it. At some point, it was the collective projection of a place that ensured it would deliver that expectation, and that feedback loop was generated by one's outlook on the place. Because of my anticipation of creative culture in Buenos Aires, maybe it was inevitable that I would find inspiration there.

~

Rita brought me upstairs to a warm, well-lit parlour hung with her paintings, most of which she had brought with her from Sydney.

I haven't been motivated to paint since I came here, she said. Now it's just the drawing class.

The house had twenty-foot-high ceilings, giving the impression that it was taller than it was wide. A narrow hall led from the parlour past two bedrooms into the kitchen. The rooms had been renovated so that the trim of the windows and doors was made of deep, burnished wood and the curtains, which were thin enough that yellow streetlight shone through them, were mounted on brass fixtures. The house had been given a fresh start, resuscitated from what had been, years before, a steady decline into shadow and rubble. The abundant light had chased away the past.

At the back of the kitchen a steep, winding staircase led up to a studio where Rita's drawings from the class were scattered on a table. There was a large brick *asado* where her husband, Manuel, was turning pieces of chicken on the grill. Knowing he was from Paraguay, I greeted him in Spanish, wanting to pay tribute to the language that was hosting us, him for a lifetime and me for just a few years, to acknowledge that there was something synonymous with being a guest in a language and being a guest in someone's house. He replied in English. His voice and his face matched each other as if they were both made of leather. He put down the metal tongs he was using to turn the chicken and gestured with a slow hand toward the door that led onto the patio.

We stepped outside into the night. The *asado* had been ingeniously designed so that it could be tended from inside the studio in the winter and from outside on the patio in the summer. Rita brought out two glasses of wine, one for me and one for Manuel, but Manuel shook his head. Rita told me that they danced out here in the summertime. Everything she said sounded sad.

At dinner I asked about Rita's drawings and Manuel's tango classes. I wanted it to be a pleasant evening, even if it might be pleasant for different reasons for each of us. When they mentioned what they had paid to buy the house two years ago, I put down my fork and had another drink of wine.

You couldn't buy a one-bedroom basement apartment with that money in Vancouver, I said.

Nor in Sydney, said Rita heavily.

It was the only evening in Buenos Aires that I spent in the English language. Soon enough the words came easily, too easily, and maybe that was why I never did it again until I was back in Canada. Part of why I was in Buenos Aires was to move deeper into language, burrowing, so that I could join it from the inside. Speaking English was time spent elsewhere, taking me away from my purpose, taking me out of the city entirely. Language was a place. I wanted to be here.

More than that, though, language was a way of being in the world. Knowing that way of being required commitment and a certain measured loneliness. I had to find out who I was in Spanish – to hear myself, to write myself, as Antón Arrufat had told me years ago in Havana. By speaking English I went rushing back to an identity that had been formed by a long relationship with the language I was born into. My relationship with Spanish, on the other hand, began more recently. I had come into it consciously.

That night, my English was halting. I spoke to Rita and Manuel with an accent, not my Canadian accent or a Spanish accent but as though English were my second language. My sentences were box-shaped. There were discernible spaces between my words. I made compact sentences without sub-clauses. I said things like, "This is what I know," and "You are generous, you are good," taking up a directness that I rarely have when I have had time to adjust to English. I pronounced all the sounds that should be pronounced, which might be why I sounded so odd.

It reminded me of a traveller speaking English, someone who had lived in many countries but felt at home in none of them. Maybe it was a kind of international English. It might have been because Rita's accent was Australian and Manuel's was a mix of Paraguayan and Australian and I was caught somewhere in the middle, another constellation in the hundreds of ways that English can be spoken and still be English.

Through the course of the evening, my English changed with wine and use. Soon I was talking out of control – not that I was talking a lot, because one could say a lot and still mean what one said, having strong ties to the words and their private meaning, but out of control in the sense that I spoke without certainty. I used words as I remembered using them weeks ago but now they felt unreliable. It was dangerous to communicate so fluidly. I tried on words like trying on shoes, looking at them down the length of my body, turning them this way and that or walking around the room in them, only realizing after I had spoken that they were too tight, too flappy, or that they squeaked. English was both pinched and spacious. There was too much room to move around in it. I couldn't find its limits and so eventually had to hold myself back from sprinting all over the conversation. I was shaken by this other way of being that seemed to belong more to the words than to me.

What I could offer my hosts in return for their warmth was a hospitality we could share, that of being hosted by language together. It would have made no sense to speak Spanish with them – that was the very exclusion that Rita encountered every day she ventured out – and I could forgo the chance to discover some aspect of myself by knowing them in Spanish. Strangely, though, it was hard to remember what we said that night, other than a few phrases, since a language that came easily went easily, too.

When it was time to go, we embraced and kissed on the cheek in the doorway. It was midnight. I asked if it was safe. They glanced at each other.

Yes, yes, it's safe, said Manuel.

I hurried across the street, turning once to wave back at them as they stood at the window, and climbed the empty hill up to Avenida San Juan. I was bursting when I reached the bright lights, suddenly thrilled by the generosity of strangers and by a city where such a welcome was possible. I called Gloria, who was just coming out of a concert with a friend, and told her I had had a marvellous night and I didn't want it to end.

Language returned, language that had built the city as much as stones and cement. Gloria laughed and told me where to meet them.

~

Many of the metaphors I was finding configured creativity as an object – either a possession in the form of an attribute, or a collection of possibilities. It was part of a bigger metaphor: *ideas are objects*. When the mathematician Henri Poincare (1854–1912) referred to "swarms of ideas" from which he selected "the most promising ones" according to aesthetic criteria,[57] he was implying that metaphor. So was the philosopher Irving Singer (1925–2015) when he wrote that the creative person was "in effect, a pack rat of creative possibilities made available to him [sic] by his sheer retention of vivid fragments amassed throughout the immediate flow of his personal life."[58] Mental processes in general and creativity in particular were based on retrieval, association, synthesis, transformation, analogical transfer, or categorical reduction – all working on the assumption that ideas were things that could be quantified, isolated, combined, or developed.

If this were true, it wasn't all bad. Treating an idea as an object meant it could be manipulated. A problem could be solved by tactical means. By moving ideas around, placing them in different relationships with one another, dividing them, combining them, one might come to "see" the problem in a different "light." Faced with a challenge, one might be encouraged to think backward, turn the situation upside down, put the problem aside, or shift one's perspective. Each tactic suggested a slightly different metaphorical engagement with the problem. Thinking backward implied retracing the causal chain of an algorithmic metaphor; putting the problem aside suggested an incubation metaphor. But no matter how varied they seemed, they were still based on the assumption that ideas were discrete objects. More than that, they configured the person who had the idea as separate from his or her own mental activity – the thinker *had* a thought. It followed that thoughts could be looked at, traded, valued, even bought and sold. Ephemera of the mind became examinable the same way flowers and rocks were examinable. The world was made of things. Let ideas be things, too. But what happened when creativity became a commodity?

So far in my search, creativity meant being productive, not reproductive.[59] If it reproduced what already existed, maybe it wasn't creative. Newness and novelty were of the highest value.[60] This view led to an economic model of creativity that had become especially popular in developed Western countries. People like urban-studies theorist Richard Florida (1957–) suggested that creativity was a market commodity.[61] He even went so far as to say that creativity identified an entire class of society, giving the haunting impression that the so-called creative class could be enumerated and accounted for. Creative capital generated new products for the market, even new markets themselves.

But there were huge risks in commodifying a human characteristic. People became instruments of the market. Creativity from an economic perspective was reduced to market viability. If the market said no, it wasn't creative. Was that the world I inhabited? Had grand narratives of meaning been replaced by economic principles?

~

The streets were empty. Grey light fell over the sidewalk through slow clouds. Somewhere in the city there was a soccer match.

Only after walking for hours did I understand that I was hungry. Most places were closed with gates pulled down over the front while others had metal bars and padlocks. I found a bakery where the door was still open and a television high up on the wall was showing the match. A portly man who looked like the owner because of the way he stood and because of the dirty white towel he had tucked into his belt was watching it with one hand resting on the back of a chair.

I asked him for two *empanadas* and a beer.

He repeated my order in a curious way, leaving out the consonants. His eyebrows were high on his forehead even when he looked down, freezing his expression in a permanent state of surprise. I sat under the television and watched the match while I ate.

Beer, good, said the owner from across the bakery. He tipped his thumb up in the air to drink from it.

I lifted the can a little off the table and put it back down, nodding. I looked back at the television. His voice was odd.

Are you for River? He pointed at the TV.

I shrugged.

It's not my team, I said.

It's not, he grimaced. Nor mine. He wagged his finger in the air as he spoke. What *is* your team?

I don't have one.

You don't? he said, visibly astonished.

I shrugged again. I knew what was about to happen. Everyone here had a team.

Where are you from?

Canada, I said.

Ah, Canada! The owner was visible thrilled. ¡Claudia! He shouted into the kitchen. *¡Canadiense!*

Claudia came rushing out, wiping her hands on her apron, looking left and right but mostly up as though she might find me somewhere in the ceiling. She had thick glasses. Her hands were contorted and her eyes rolled back and forth without settling.

The man I had been talking to introduced himself as Carlos. He presented his wife, Claudia, and said that she was mute. He put his hand over his mouth when he said it, then spread his hands out in the air to demonstrate that something had stopped. I realized then why his voice sounded odd: he was mute, too, but not as mute as Claudia. The fact that they had found each other filled me with tenderness.

Carlos wanted to know if there were *empanadas* in Canada and how much did they cost. When I told him yes but they were expensive he repeated the question and my answer to Claudia, who nodded vigorously. Claudia looked at me without blinking. Carlos repeated everything I had said with the same words and big gestures while Claudia rattled her approval with constant nodding.

Using mostly gestures and signs, Carlos explained that he and Claudia met when they were eight years old. His mother drove a bus and she would drive them both to school. He walked around the bakery picking up invisible children and putting them in an invisible basket in his lap, as though each child were the size of a loaf of bread.

Un pibe acá, he demonstrated, *otro pibe acá*. One kid here, another kid here. *Otro, otro*, until he wiped his hands together in the air and said he had asked Claudia to marry him. He said he was very lucky that she agreed. At that time they were both twenty-six.

Now he was sixty-five. I nodded, seeing that they understood each other in a way that any couple would envy. They had two daughters, Carlos added, and with a pride that melted my heart, his hands on his hips and his chin tilted up, his eyes widening even more than I thought possible, announced that neither one of them was mute.

Oido perfecto, he said, kissing his fingertips and opening his hand in the air to let the kiss free. Perfect hearing. Then he turned to Claudia and repeated everything he had told me, to which Claudia nodded, thrilled.

By the time I left the bakery that afternoon, Carlos had shown me the scar behind his ear where some sort of hearing device had been surgically installed and later removed because it made him too sensitive to the tiniest sound.

I don't have to hear everything, he said. Just what's important.

He had unbuttoned his shirt, too, and shown me the scar where he had had open-heart surgery after a heart attack nine years ago. He was retired now but didn't want to sit around at home watching TV. With the bakery at least, there was work to be done.

I was suddenly sleepy, as if the city were commanding me to dream. I thanked Carlos for the *empanadas* and dragged myself to Lezama Park where I lay on the grass. A man asked me for money. I sat up and told him I didn't have any, which is the way I had heard other people say it, *no tengo*, and *disculpa*, forgive me, accompanied by a small shrug and a squint. Many times I had seen a woman camped on Avenida Callao across from the Plaza Rodríguez Peña, wrapped in blankets, and to each person who said *disculpa*, forgive me, to her outstretched hand she said, *disculpado*, forgiven. I had never heard that particular reply before. She had elevated the moment, giving it dignity. Knowing the words was easy but knowing when to say them took listening.

The man left me alone on the grass. I read a book for an interview I would do in a couple of days, but only some of the sentences sunk in, only a few of them meant anything. The rest was just noise. At the bottom of the park, a dog chased pigeons until it caught one, the dog's owner jogging after it and shouting half-heartedly, but the dog had already devoured the bird and bloody feathers hung from its mouth.

~

One of the most prevalent metaphors for creativity in the twentieth and twenty-first centuries was the *boundary* metaphor.[62] Creativity meant trespassing into a new territory, pushing beyond a border. It meant exploring beyond the familiar and breaking with the past.[63] When someone said, "Think outside the box," they meant, *think beyond conventional ways of considering this problem*, intimating, too, that convention was a container.

The boundary metaphor was explicitly territorial. It set limits to the spatiality of what was known, and construed creativity as rupturing that limit to encounter the mystery beyond. It was politically derived – being able to redraw a map meant taking new territory for one's own.[64] When action ventured into unknown territory, it planted a flag, the flag of creative work, declaring that someone had been there and that the territory was no longer foreign. From then on, the same idea would not be novel. It presumed that dynamic action took place at the margins, by trespassing beyond those margins into new and uncharted lands. In short, the creative person redrew the borders of knowledge.

Like every metaphor, the boundary metaphor obscured as much as it revealed. First, it was obsessed with outcomes. Like colonization, only the planting of new flags mattered. It didn't matter how one got there or what happened along the way.

Second, the boundary metaphor couldn't account for the flux of circumstance. By noticing only trespasses into new territory, it was insensitive to the way that knowledge was constantly being reordered, reworked, recalibrated, or "*re*discovered." To continue the metaphor, if all eyes were on the border, no one would notice the changes back home.

Third, crossing a creative boundary was usually attributed retrospectively.[65] The artist, or the surrounding society, looked back and realized that a boundary had been crossed. But if creativity could be recognized only in retrospect, how could one examine creativity as a process? The boundary metaphor implied that knowledge meant acquisition, entailing mastery of a domain or controlling a territory.[66] The knower was lord of his or her territory in a grab for more land, more knowledge, acquired through creative skirmishes with the unknown.

~

My drawings were terrible. I couldn't emulate the instructor's way of working, which relied on finding the right line in the first mark of the charcoal, as if he were tracing a drawing that was already there. Instead, I blocked out large areas of light and shadow, building them up until they met at a sharp contrast. He didn't like it. The result was stylistically too predictable. But there was only so much I could learn at once, and I had chosen language, creativity, and Buenos Aires. Maybe another time I would choose drawing. I stopped going to class.

A week later, I ran into the instructor on the street. I wanted to turn around and walk the other way before he saw me. I was ashamed that I had given up, but it was too late. He teetered in the wind.

Tanto tiempo, joven, he said without slowing. So much time, young man.

For an instant the many walls he had painted as a muralist flashed upward behind him, as though the murals extended from his wispy hair. I felt the colour blue and sunlight on the paint and could see the texture of the bricks. Then they vanished and the street was full of loud grey cars again. We walked side by side.

I still had no desire to return to the class. But could I interview him? It would be good to hear about the metaphors he used, and besides, he was famous. A young woman had come to one of the classes, at first, I thought, to draw, but she cleaned up her easel and put away her materials before the class was over and waited until the instructor sighed, *bueno, hija*, what questions did you want to ask me? At which point the girl produced a notepad and wrote down his short replies, nodding constantly.

The thought of interviewing him, a thought that occurred as an image of a conversation imbued with privilege, suddenly weighed me down. He didn't like to talk, after all, and I was already sorry. It wasn't a good place to begin. More importantly, though, my interviews weren't really about specific questions I wanted answered as much as they were a way of being in the company of someone I would otherwise have no way of being with, of sharing something through purposeful conversation. There wasn't anything in particular I wanted to know, at least not concretely, just things I wanted to feel through the exchange of language. The best interviews I had done were with people who wanted to talk. He wasn't one of those.

I stammered an apology for not coming to class. I've been busy, I said.

Of course, you have, he shrugged.

It's up to you, he added. I have to go to the bank.

I considered standing by the glass door while he went inside to the bank machine, guarding the entrance. It seemed appropriate given the general fear of robbery that pervaded the city, but he knew infinitely more than I did about how to live here.

When we parted, shame clung to me like the smell of bad meat.

~

Was creativity transferable across domains? Were there many creativities – one for the composer, another for the mathematician – or were they connected by something in common? Could drawing make me a better writer? The metaphor of an *amusement park* highlighted some of the interdisciplinary overlap that went on between creative activities.[67]

The amusement park emphasized a socio-cultural perspective. Its vision wasn't focused on the individual's experience of creativity. If it was about the individual, it would include the perspective of the person who visited the amusement park – how did they navigate the rides? How did they choose which one they liked most? How would they compare their experience of different rides? But those considerations were easier understood from the testimonials of creative people. To understand creativity among the domains, the amusement park looked to its structural aspects.

For example, the phrase "You must be this high to ride"[68] helped to understand the relationship between intellect and creativity (as an aside, it could also be taken as a comment on the relationship between drugs and art). One had to have a minimum level of intelligence and motivation, as well as a suitable environment, to develop one's creativity. The level of intelligence varied depending on the domain – for example, higher intelligence was required for mathematical creativity than painting. However, after a certain level, higher intelligence made little difference to creative potential, and in some cases an extremely high level of intelligence could inhibit creativity because there was simply too much to draw on and the artist was overwhelmed.[69]

Continuing the metaphor, a phrase like "Now that we're in Tomorrowland, where do we find Space Mountain?" alluded to specific tasks, or microdomains. It pointed to assumptions that were often made about domain similarity, fancying that one kind of creativity (one kind of ride at the amusement park) was grouped within a larger one. A closer look revealed that there were nuanced differences between each ride, even though they might have shared some thematic common ground. Applied to creativity, it meant that an umbrella domain entailed specific and diverse subsets. For example, painting drew on different talents than sculpting, even though both were creative engagements with aesthetic experience. When it came to writing, it was the same. There were many forms, from journalism to recipe books to literary fiction, each making use of language yet each with its own expertise.

~

I wrote notes at the Bar de Cao on Avenida Independencia until Gloria came to collect me. We rode the subway to her class at the university. The A Line had been built in 1913, the first on the continent, and the wooden doors still had to be pulled apart by hand. Julio Cortázar had lived along this route. I touched an old leather strap that held the window down, just in case he had touched it too.

Classes were long. Three hours of listening emptied my stomach and with it my concentration. I clung to people's words as though the room were water and language were the only thing that floated. When it was over, I was exhausted from trying to smile and laugh at the right times. Defeated, I bought Gloria and me a snack at a café across the street. My Spanish improved with the food and the company so that I could once again float on top of my sentences.

That night I went alone to a *taller* for aspiring writers, a workshop that the boyfriend of a friend-of-a-friend had invited me to. I stood below the door on a dark street at the address I had been given. A few cars passed at the distant ends. When I buzzed the apartment, a man's voice asked me to wait. Others were just about to arrive; he didn't want to come down twice. I scuffed my shoes on the broken sidewalk under the pale-yellow streetlight, wondering if it was safer to stand in the light or the shadow, to show who I was or to hide it. When a few minutes had passed, I was joined by a small, thin woman.

Are you here for the fiction workshop? I asked.

Yes, you too? she said.

My heart opened with a belonging that I only knew from glimpses of the world as a place of outsiders, all wishing for someone or something to make us feel at home. I was not alone after all. Three more people arrived. Matías appeared, the voice from the buzzer, and we climbed the stairs to his apartment.

That night, time was different: three hours passed like minutes. We drank *mate*, ate biscuits, talked about what made a good story, and critiqued the work that people had written in the week since the last meeting. Spanish came more easily now, although I was still missing something when I read. In English I saw beyond the words, as if language were a wall made of a thousand tiny windows through which I could see experience made fresh; but when I read stories in Spanish I saw the windows themselves – partly because the frames of the windows, the words, their sounds and their echoes, were so pretty – and only with a focus that was both earnest and relaxed could I see what was beyond them, the bigger sense of place on the other side. In the best moments, though, which were also the simplest, I held my papers like everyone else, felt the quiet rush of insight or humour, and let go of time as it passed. That was enough to feel at home, and when Matías asked after a silent spell, *Adrián, ¿qué pensás?* What do you think? I was surprised, then relieved, then encouraged that I had something to say after all.

I wanted to walk home when the workshop was over but there was one section near El Once that people said was not safe. So I resorted to the subway. The journey would have taken an hour and a half on foot, but by subway it was ten minutes, during which I missed all of the city – the yellow light on the buildings in winter, the scarves and the clop of boots. I came above ground at San Juan station to walk the last blocks home. Eugenio had already eaten. He sat at the table, smoking cigarettes while I chewed my steak, and asked what I had learned since yesterday. I replied: the revelation that Buenos Aires was named not after good winds, though the winds that blew through the city were indeed good, coming in from the pampas, but after the patron saint of sailors, the Virgin of Buen Ayre; the snippets of Lunfardo, playful dockside slang unique to the city, that I had absorbed, like *feka* for *café* or *vesre* for *revés* (reverse); and something I had read by the Argentine-Canadian Alberto Manguel, that Buenos Aires, like all great cities, didn't exist "except in the memory of those who live or lived there."[70]

It's real enough to me, Eugenio shrugged.

He explained the names for different cuts of beef and teased me for what he called the *monarquía de cartón*, the cardboard monarchy, that we have in Canada. I took clandestine photos of him with my phone. Seeing him made me happy, and having the pictures meant I could draw him, a tribute to his peculiar grace.

That night I couldn't sleep. I lay awake thinking of something Gloria had said that afternoon in the café: You seem to like it here so much, why don't you live in Buenos Aires for a while? I could pass you my apartment when I leave. You could write and draw, keep going with the interviews. Maybe that's what you need.

She was right, I thought, wanting to stay in the city of my dreams. But how long would those dreams last?

~

Even if a lot of metaphors assumed that ideas were objects, there were variations in the kind of objects meant. One example was that ideas were containers, as in the phrase "think outside the box." Another container metaphor was that creativity was an *investment.* Creativity meant buying low and selling high when it came to putting one's time, energy, and skill into an idea.[71]

Even though the investing model of creativity was developed in the late twentieth century, economic metaphors had been used to describe the workings of creativity long before that.[72] It entailed taking risks by giving attention to marginalized and unpopular ideas and developing them until they matured into something desirable. One had to move toward ideas that were under-used or under-acknowledged and dedicate one's self to those, implying a defiance of what was already considered creative. Invariably, one risked social alienation when ignoring the crowd – one could suffer derision and be ostracized.[73] The key to the investment metaphor for creativity was to persevere through alienation and commit to the marginalized idea because of some personal belief in its worth, trusting that its very exclusion from popularity now was what laid the foundation for its value in the future.[74]

Creativity, then, was largely a decision, one that could be based on empirical research, to determine which ideas were unpopular and which ones had potential for higher value. It relied on making rational assessments and following through on the results of one's findings. It didn't mean that creativity was as simple as finding unpopular ideas and sticking with them. That was not true for all un-popular ideas – some ideas remained unpopular no matter how much work one put into them. But it did point to the important role of reason, lucidity, and assessment in the creative process. One could *decide* to generate new ideas and examine them. To this end, creativity constituted an act of will as much as an act of intu-ition. Creativity was a risk taken in the interest of gain.

~

I killed time in Plazoleta Cortázar in Palermo. I was early for an interview, and sat across from the swings with my back against the low stone wall in the roundabout, reading a collection of stories by Vanesa Guerra. A group of teenagers set up drums and played flutes and shakers in a way that reminded me of Bolivia. The sun went down with the late yellow light falling into my lap, then moving across the low wall of the park until only the musicians were lit and the street was cast in one broad shadow from the buildings. People came to sit on the half-wall, dangling one leg over the side with the other leg crossed in front of them on the cement while they looked into their phone, wrote something, rested their phone on their thigh, and looked up at the teenagers playing music, then, after a pause, looked down at their phone again in a pattern they repeated until someone arrived and their faces lit up, they kissed on the cheek, and walked away together. A woman sat on the ground with her back against the wall not far from where I was reading, one leg crossed over the other in front of her, and read a book whose title I could not see. I resolved to say hello if she was still there when I got up, but the more I thought about it the emptier I felt so that there was nothing in the world I could offer except silence and space, which surely was all she wanted. I imagined her stopping at a bar to meet friends on her way home. I imagined their familiarity, their laughter.

Places in Buenos Aires were always being re-placed, a bar was once a café that was once a bookstore that was once a shop that fixed watches. Even though the places themselves were gone, they persisted in the ones they became, auras, ghosts, borrowed memories, so that the city advanced into modernity at the same time that it regressed into nostalgia. The city was all the cities it had been. I could feel them without being able to name them. And yet I couldn't find the aching traces of what was there before the city was founded, the pampas that met the River Plate and the people that had roamed where cars now rumbled over broken asphalt. My indentured nostalgia went back a hundred years and then it stopped. I would have to leave the city, go south, go inland, to understand what was there before the city. It was a journey I would not make, not this time. One day.

I stopped pretending to read and folded the book over my knee, looking up at the teenagers and their music, seeing that they were ragged as if they had been travelling. I couldn't tell if they had known each other for years or for the length of a song. They didn't pass around a hat or a cup for money when they finished, but let the music collapse into a tinkle of laughter as the sun left the plaza, the light slipping up the tree trunks into the branches and easing into the pale blue sky that now seemed bitten or stung by street lights. They packed up their drums and sat on a bench, taking turns drinking from a clear, label-less plastic bottle while a girl with tattoos on her arms came and went, talking to someone across the plaza and then returning to the bench for another drink. They walked away with their drums on their back when the bottle was empty. The woman who had been reading beside me was gone. I zipped up my jacket. It was the time of day that the famous Argentine writer Ernesto Sábato (1911–2011) described in his novel *Sobre Héroes y Tumbas (On Heroes and Tombs)*: "Darkness falls. And everything is different: the trees, the benches … the far off echo of the city. That hour when everything enters upon a more profound, more enigmatic existence. And a more fearful one as well for the solitary beings who at that hour continue to sit, silent and pensive, on the benches of the plazas and parks of Buenos Aires."[75] I was alone in the grey dusk of a city that knew nothing about me, cast into a void, with only the scant outline of plans to keep me from blowing away entirely.

After the interview, I zigzagged back and forth through Palermo in the early night between Calle Thames and Scalabrini Ortíz, wishing there was someone I could call. I sat on the half-wall in the plaza again and checked my phone as though a friend would be there any minute, even looked up and scanned the clumps of people that moved by in the yellow-tinted shadows across the street with what I thought was an expectant, hopeful expression. The cement was cold. I thought of the woman who had been reading in the late afternoon and of the many good conversations she was having. When I couldn't pretend any longer, I pushed off from the wall as if it were an island and I was going out to sea. Walking made sense, more sense than sitting still, as though walking were a place all to itself. Walking, reading, and writing – all of them were places.

I reached the subway station at Santa Fe and checked the map. I could walk back to Constitución, resting at bookstores along the way. It would take only a couple of hours, and besides, I had all the time in the world.

~

What if creativity was an *organism*? It was still a thing, but it could grow. It was in a continual process of becoming,[76] and it required the active participation of its caregiver – the person who gave birth to or nurtured the creative work. That would mean a parallel metaphor: creativity was *transformation*.[77] It implied that creativity was a relation more than an outcome, reconfiguring a problem not only so that it could be seen differently but so that it could become something different, too. That metaphor cropped up in descriptions like this: "an individual creative mind is more like a tended garden, in which seeds of memes are sown ... and sprouting memes are subjected to selective weeding and cultivation."[78] It didn't have to be so specifically evoked as a garden. It could include biological processes more generally, like cooperation, interaction, birth, growth, or evolution, as I had already discovered, applied to ideas just as they were to the natural world. It was an inside-outside process, meaning that the idea began in the individual and had the potential to grow beyond the parent that gave birth to it.[79] It was a contrast to the boundary metaphor, an outside-inside process, whereby the creative person ventured into new territory and made it familiar by bringing it into one's self, into the realm of the known. The organism was a good antithesis to the boundary for another reason, too: while the boundary meant that creativity happened at the fringes and was focused on outcomes, the organism situated creativity at the centre and focused on process. By acknowledging time as a constitutive part of creativity, the organism metaphor made room for a world in constant motion and flux – an accommodation that the boundary metaphor had a hard time making because it presumed that nothing new was happening at home. To re-till the soil of the garden metaphor, creativity was a process that "operat[ed] through principles of time-dependant vitality comparable to those in trees and shrubs."[80]

Whether boundary or organism, I was coming to understand that no metaphor worked alone. There were always multiple active metaphors, each one modifying the meaning of creativity. For example, looking closely at a creative process revealed a series of micro-boundaries, small episodes of breakthroughs that, when viewed from a distance, resembled a punctuated equilibrium marking the growth of an idea.[81] On the other side, the breakthroughs that characterized the boundary metaphor might have been a product of preparation, or were nurtured and combined with other ideas already at the fringe, or they lay in wait until their time came.

~

During the day I walked through the city, and during the night I dreamed of it. I floated over the sidewalk of Entre Ríos in alternating patches of light and dark, yellow from the street lamps and a deep-purple bruise from the shadows of trees, while cars and sometimes *colectivos* drifted past. There was a *parilla* I had never tried but it was always crowded, with people spilling onto the sidewalk most nights until two o'clock in the morning. In the window of my mind the restaurant was so smoky that the room with all its families was filled with a pale blue cloud. From there I leapt to the neighbourhood of Boedo and walked north in my memory, which was now as much a fantasy as it was any part of the past, floating up Castro Barros Avenue until it became Medrano to linger in patches of thought that lit the place more than the lights did.

I imagined the members of my writing workshop arriving at a meeting as though all at once along Medrano, knowing at the same time that they came one by one from different directions. Pilar, then Ivan, then Paula, passed under a streetlamp, the glare catching on a red sash that Pilar used to tie back her hair and glinting, in a different time that was somehow the same time, on the rim of Ivan's glasses. I could see the brighter light of Avenida Rivadavia shining on the skin on the top of Pablo's head as he walked up the stairs from Castro Barros subway station.

What were they doing now? Their homes were scattered across the city like a handful of dice. In my mind they were all the same: they lived alone in tiled second-floor apartments, with scant furniture so that it was possible to trace the line where the floor met the wall almost all the way around the room, except where it was interrupted by a single couch and the four legs of a writing table, and from each of their homes a yellow rectangle of light shone out above the street, the kind of light that I would see from down below as I walked and wondered, looking up, if it was theirs.

I hid in the corner of their lives, wishing we could share a night and a bottle of wine. But I didn't know where to find them – not just in the city but in their hearts. They were complete without me, they had everything they needed, friends and family, routines and fears, plans and hopes of their own. Even their surprises were regulated by a different system. Spanish and a shared taste for books was only part of a language. Everything I considered doing to intervene seemed to go against the natural rhythm of the city, as though I were constantly striving to silence my part in it at the same time that I wanted to sing. Maybe if I braved the dark pass under the bridge that divided Constitución from San Cristóbal, turning on San Juan then heading north on Entre Ríos, I could find myself in the light of memory, equal to the light of nostalgia, and that, curiously, had something to do with hope ...

~

One of the most satisfying states of creative immersion was *flow*. Artists knew it. So did athletes. It meant operating at peak performance in total engagement with the activity. It happened when the goal was clear, the activity itself seemed to offer feedback, the artist or athlete felt that their personal skills were matched to the task, they achieve intense focus, a loss of self-awareness, and an altered sense of time.[82] The work itself became intrinsically rewarding.

The flow metaphor emphasized interactionism. It wasn't just a product of the individual, but of the relationship between the individual and their environment. It meant maintaining a delicate balance between anxiety and boredom. Too far in either direction and flow was lost.

I came across a pertinent study of flow as it related to creative writing. Poets and fiction writers were asked if they had experienced a sense of losing track of time while writing.[83] Altered temporality was integral to the state of flow. Short answer: they did. But along the way, peripheral to the goals of the research, respondents revealed a constellation of metaphors for creativity. Some of the novelists described moving into a movie screen, peeling layers, opening a faucet. Some of the poets described tapping a vein, diving underwater, becoming a pulse, surfing a wave, and feeling one's way into the skin of the work. These were the kinds of nuanced, spoken metaphors I wanted more of.

~

The dream of the night went on. As if from far away, I watched my foot go into my shoe and my arms disappear into my jacket. I heard my soles scuff down the cement steps and my hand pat my pockets for keys, phone, and money. The bolt of the door clanged. In the words of the Argentine novelist Silvina Bullrich (1915–1990), in the opening to her 1939 novel *Calles de Buenos Aires* (The Streets of Buenos Aires): "To say city was to say insomnia."[84]

Up ahead I recognized the family that lived in the darkness under the bridge. Two men stood talking by the cement wall, one with his arms crossed and the other with his leg hitched up on a cinder block, his pants too short, one shoe without a sock. Three people slept on the mattress against the wall, their backs to the street. I could see that two of them were very small, their bodies curved like half-moons wrapped in blankets, and a woman sat up between them with more blankets over her lap, looking up sometimes to speak in a low voice to the men who stood nearby.

I held my breath and did not know how to pass them, then decided that I should pass them breathing. My body tensed, moving into a moment where possibilities shattered outward, even terrible ones that I could imagine but not accept. The sound of fear in my head was sharp and shrill. When I drifted by without incident, it faded and grew lower like the siren of a passing ambulance.

With the shadow of the overpass at my back, the narrow point of my mind opened: the man with his foot hitched up on the cinder block might have been a friend of theirs who had just stopped by for a chat, passing time on a Thursday night. The family would one day remember the corner the same way I remembered the home I grew up in, as a place with its cycles of weather, accident, and feelings of community. They would look back on it from a day that didn't exist yet as one of the many places they had lived, or even as one of the few places they had lived, and they would remember it in a way that no one else could. They were the custodians of memories I would never have.

Their faces in the blast of headlights from the occasional car that passed under the bridge and their hands in the shadows of the blankets seemed suddenly important, even necessary, as though without them the bridge would collapse. I thought of a story by Jorge Luis Borges, "Tlön, Uqbar, Orbis Tertius," in which memory kept a place alive so that a few birds were all that protected a certain amphitheatre from vanishing. Then I wanted to tell the family I was sorry: sorry for being afraid of them, sorry for comparing their hard life to a story that I found beautiful, as if beauty were enough to live on, even if it was, for me, enough to live for.

Avenida Entre Ríos was empty. A fog had settled along Belgrano. The door to the *parilla* was closed and all the tables inside were full, as though it had brought in what it wanted of the night and left the rest on the street to get cold. Strange mannequins stared wide-eyed and stiff from dark dress shops. I hurried across the shadowy expanse between the plaza and the National Congress.

Corrientes was an oasis of light. I stood on the corner of Callao against a metal door that had been pulled down over one of the bookstores and watched people parade by, envying and celebrating their friendship. It was dazzling to be alone among so many people at night. I walked in the direction of the obelisk as colossal theatres spilled lives onto the sidewalk between blankets laid out on the cement where other lives sold scarves, plug adaptors, umbrellas, and batteries.

From the obelisk I walked back on the other side of Corrientes, feeling safe as long as I stayed in the light of the busy avenue, knowing that the rest of the city was darkening. At the back of a bookstore near Callao, a man was reciting poems while a woman played guitar between his verses. She had a strong angular face; his was round and always upturned, pleading. When he finished each poem, he came back down from his residency in the ceiling as though his own smile had broken him, looking bewildered to find that a room full of people had been listening. After the zenith of one of his poems he raised up his arms from his sides and finished, saying, *la vida es …*, then hesitated with his arms still in the air. I was sure he was going to say some sort of metaphor and I was even prepared to wince – life is a flower, life is a doorway, life is an egg – but instead the pattern of language transformed and he said … *lo mejor que yo conozco* … the best that I know, finishing the phrase in a way that made me feel refreshed and humble.

Could I have shared this with anyone? Would I have known how?

I went back into the night, moving briskly over the wide space where the sky sagged low in front of the Congress building. The streetlights grew farther apart. Now the *parilla* was closed and the chairs were upside down on the tables in the dark. The fog that had begun at Belgrano made the street uncertain, vague and abrupt, with the shapes of two young men appearing suddenly beneath the awning of a gas station, crossing into the soft yellow air to fade as the headlights of a car drifted over their wake. I saw myself as if from across the street, a hunched little boy powering through the night on skinny legs, his neck down as though something would drop on him at any minute from one of the balconies. Stand up! I urged him, and felt the weight of my arms relax into my jacket. I lifted my head and took the time to walk properly, with care and purpose, but not abandon, not teetering on the brink of a sprint. For that moment I was safe, and the next moment, too. My fear was for things that hadn't happened.

I breathed into the fog, passing a shoe store and the butcher shop. A tiny bar on the corner of Entre Ríos and San Juan was still open. The owner and his son were watching soccer on a TV that was stacked on top of the fridge. I asked for a beer and sat at a small wooden table by the door, writing a list of all the things I would miss about this place. The list became a letter that I would read out loud at the writing workshop to tell the others what it meant for me to be there.

When I passed under the bridge on my way back to the house I held my breath, then remembered to breathe. The family was fast asleep.

~

Creativity didn't have to be a thing. Couldn't it also be a relation? And what if it was a political relation? Maybe creativity was a kind of *democratic attunement*.[85]

By this metaphor, creativity meant an awareness of the productive tension between traditional opposites like freedom and discipline, intellect and intuition, individuality and unity.[86] People often assumed that these opposites were incompatible, or that one would overcome the other. But democracy proposed a model whereby interacting with both ends of polar opposites was productive and even essential to a healthy society. Attending to that tension was a kind of Janusian thinking, holding two or more opposing thoughts in mind without conflict – a little like metaphor itself, which relied on bringing together two separate identities. Creativity, then, was simultaneously a "bid for freedom and an application of discipline."[87] In other words, the individual needed freedom to express him or herself, but that expression had to be situated in a context of discipline if it was to mean anything. It was like Lorca's "wild horses, flexible reins" from his essay on the *duende*. Nietzsche explored these two contrasting influences that descended from the ancient Greeks – Apollonian influences like sanity, security, and level-headedness, and Dionysian influences like instinct, intuition, and transgression. Neither one dominated. Instead, creativity arose from the way each opposite kept the other honest, maintaining a balance. It was like the angel and the demon, but instead of listening to one, the creative person listened to both. The angel made the demon demonic while the demon pushed the angel to higher virtue. The creative act was the productive response to accounting for diverging but equally important values. It was a space between two forces but not the forces themselves. The creative person was "more primitive and more cultivated, more destructive and more constructive, occasionally crazier and yet adamantly saner, than the average person."[88] What would I have to do to maintain that precarious balance?

~

Metaphors for creativity lay scattered all around. Did anything unite them?

Whether I noticed it or not, describing one metaphor connected it to others. If creativity was democratic attunement, it was also tension. If creativity was illumination, it was also about seeing, which suggested the importance of perspective. Other metaphors contradicted each other. How many times had I read about a thought "arising" or that a thought could be "had" at all? Every verb implied a conceptual framework that often went unnoticed.

Contradiction wasn't all bad. Each metaphor revealed something important about the topic – each one illuminated certain aspects while obscuring others.[89] That was metaphor's strength, not weakness. Surveying the range showed the multiple facets of creativity, how it could be different kinds of product and different kinds of process. I didn't want to conclude with just one; I wanted to explore how it could be many things at once. But until now, I had turned my gaze to books and to myself. I needed to attend to other people's speech. I needed to hear how they understood what it meant to be creative so that I could expand my range of what was possible. This was not a search through text, but through the living voices that brought language into being every day. I had to meet with people. We had to talk about creativity. I had to really listen, and that was where the conversations with writers began.

~

The Metaphor Metaphor:
From Experience to
Language and Back Again

But first, a pause in the interval.

Metaphor was a noun. It was a thing. "Can you find the metaphors in this sonnet?" "How many are there?" Configuring it as a noun emphasized its remoteness from other nouns. It divided language neatly into units – metaphors could be enumerated, sorted, and categorized. That focus on quantification was especially strong in Western languages like English and Spanish. Indigenous languages didn't seem so attached to the *things* of language or divide them up so emphatically. Instead, *relations* between things were the emphasis.[1] The problem was that by expressing that idea in English, I had forced myself into an epistemological orientation that focused again on the things.

I wanted to use metaphor as a verb. I would still use its property as a noun to get there, collecting and examining metaphors as if they were precious stones. But I believed that metaphor was more than a range of objects. It was a way of thinking. It might even have been thinking itself. Creativity, another noun, was just a means for reaching that deeper way of thought.

Like most ideas, mine wasn't new. Aristotle's *Poetics* described the capacity for thinking metaphorically.[2] It meant learning to see resemblances, but not just between two things. That was how metaphor was usually considered: Juliet is the sun. A = B. The writer, then the reader, perceived some common ground between two separate identities in the world. Those identities were named by language – "between two signs," as Jacques Derrida wrote.³ But metaphorical thinking also achieved something more profound. It was a way of considering the dynamic tension between language and experience. By living and "languaging," one brought the stuff of life into words. The irony and limitation of what I was writing was the means of expression itself – here I was, writing it, so I was still propping up Derrida's idea that language made everything into a sign. The distinction I wanted to make was between language and [experience], with square brackets around experience to make it clear that it was a stand-in for a phenomenon beyond what was written. All words were signs in relation to a world of experience – not necessarily stable, constant signs, for the meaning of words changed and varied with their use, but a system of relations held them in a temporary but useful pattern.

I had language and I had experience. How did they interact? And what did metaphor have to do with it? Language and experience weren't the same, but they affected each other. When I had an [experience] – again with square brackets because the word was a placeholder – and I wished to convey it, I brought it into something other than the experience itself. In other words, I carried it over. That was what metaphor meant: from the Greek *metapherein*, "to transfer," to bring beyond.⁴ It was also an act of translation: from the Greek *translatus*, "carried across." That was the kind of thinking I was interested in.

Derrida had some useful, if hypnotic, things to say about the relationship between experience and language, which he wrote about as a relationship between thought and metaphor:

"Thought happens upon metaphor, or metaphor is the lot of thought at the moment at which a sense attempts to emerge of itself to say itself, to express itself, to bring itself into the light of language."⁵

What was he saying? Sense, akin to [experience], emerged *through* language and *into* language, but it also emerged *by* language, becoming the expressive aspect of itself through its self-reflexive engagement with the words that brought it into being. For example,

I had an experience and it was outside language. It just *was*. To express that experience, it emerged into language. Derrida's passage created the very sensation of that emergence – the sense developed right before my eyes. The sentence transformed from abstraction into the concrete expression of language. The sentence mirrored that process, beginning with the word "thought" and ending with the word "language." It mimicked the way [experience] emerged into language.

But conveying experience into language wasn't such a linear process. When I spoke about my experience, I was reflecting on it. I was considering the experience itself and my experience of language as I had come to know it. Each experience was surrounded by a thick cloud of words, like flies, buzzing and humming. Around some experiences, there were only one or two words. Around others there were hundreds. And some experiences were without words at all. I couldn't imagine how to say them. The amount of words was never fixed. Everyone had a uniquely calibrated experience of language – no two people experience a word in exactly the same way – so no one saw the same pattern of words buzzing around an experience. Still, because of the shared nature of language, there was a lot of words in common. The same word might have referred to different experiences for each person who used it, but the conventions of language often masked those differences. Without those conventions, the world would have been a lonely place, everyone speaking a private, unintelligible language. Every time I expressed my experience, I made a choice: Which words were the best fit for what I wanted to convey? There were many more options available than the ones I took up. It was comforting to know that phrases like "this sucks" or "she's great" were ready at hand, that they imparted simple but useful meaning. But there were other words that could reflect my unique calibration of language more precisely. Selecting them carefully, I could share a special nuance of my experience and bring it uniquely into language.

For Aristotle, the ability to work with metaphor was "the mark of genius."[6] I didn't think it had to be reserved for an intellectual elite. Thinking metaphorically was a mindfulness that heightened awareness to the ways that experience and language were configured. Just as I searched outwardly to find resemblances between words to make a metaphor (in speaking metaphorically), I searched inwardly to find resemblances between language and [experience] (in thinking metaphorically).

If metaphorical thinking sounded like a lot of work, that's because it was. But since I took up language nearly every day of my life, and since it influenced how I thought, which in turn influenced how I acted, surely it was a worthy challenge.

~

Fortunately, not all speech had to be a revolutionary poetic act, even though all speech had revolutionary poetic potential. So-called "dead metaphors" were useful for conveying meaning. The phrase "dead metaphor" was, ironically, a metaphor, too. It was a metaphor that had "lost the vigour of youth, but remain[ed] a metaphor,"[7] cliché conversions of experience into language that had become commonplace. For example, a phrase like "I see what you mean" relied on the metaphors *understanding is seeing* and *ideas are objects*, even though it didn't necessarily entail ocular visibility. Saying it with one's eyes closed did not diminish its meaning. Nietzsche thought that philosophy was founded on dead metaphors.[8] Derrida seemed to think so, too. But using dead metaphors didn't mean I couldn't also contribute innovative metaphors to describe experience. For example, it was difficult to describe metaphors like "the legs of a table" or a "bottle neck" in literal terms. Looking to other languages breathed new life into what seemed at first like a dead metaphor: in French a skylight was *un puit de lumière*: a well of light. In Spanish to give birth was *dar a luz*: to give to light. Both expressions were conventional formulations in their own language but from an English perspective were richly metaphorical and novel. And wasn't there something refreshing about a table that had legs, as if it were an animal, or a road that narrowed the traffic as if it were in a bottle – or a bottle that had a neck as if it were a person?

Each metaphor was a label, attached to a thing or an event as a way of saying something about it that was, ideally, meaningful.[9] Even though they were conventional, they still animated speech in productive ways. I began to believe that there was no such thing as dead metaphors, only metaphors that people failed to notice or failed to appreciate. Maybe it was more apt to say that it wasn't the metaphor that had died, but that sensitivity to it had. Even considering alternative metaphors for the concept of dead metaphors could open up new ways of thinking about how language could be brought back to life.

But there was a problem with all of this. I could say that thinking was a process of making metaphor, but soon enough I hit a wall. In any project on metaphor, I had to consider how metaphor was a metaphor itself.[10] Claiming that metaphor was "a matter of teaching an old word new tricks"[11] defined metaphor by using metaphor, in that case *metaphor is an animal*. When Derrida wrote that metaphor "dwell[ed] in a borrowed home,"[12] he implied that *metaphor is a person*, or at least some creature capable of having an abode. The foundational tools for articulating metaphor were metaphorical, so that explaining metaphor required a whole cluster of other metaphors around it, metaphors like vehicle, tenor, frame, focus, modifier, source, and so on.[13] Even "concept" was a metaphor.[14] Metaphor was always subsuming and replacing itself, never completely resolving into literal language and existing forever in the ephemeral world of the figurative. No matter how rigorously I analyzed metaphor, there would always be outside it the metaphor for metaphor. George Lakoff and Mark Johnson thought it was proof that all thinking was metaphorical.[15] Seeing beyond metaphor was impossible. After all, there was no way to make metaphor literal: "there [was] no non-metaphorical standpoint from which one could look upon metaphor."[16]

But even if I couldn't see beyond metaphor – *thinking is seeing* – I could become more aware of metaphor by thinking metaphorically. I could develop a greater sensitivity to the way metaphors were tied to conceptual frameworks, and I could train my agency and responsibility by learning how to manipulate those conceptual frameworks. Just as meditation and mindfulness practised aware-ness of mind, using consciousness to explore how consciousness behaved, I could use metaphor to explore how metaphor behaved. In doing so, I could let go of fixed attachments to set ways of seeing the world and start to think about how things could be otherwise.

It wasn't easy. Reflecting on experience and language had to be done outside of what was written for what was written to have any meaning. Because language was conceptual, metaphorical, a world of signs, it would never be equal to experience in itself. Words moved me because they reminded me of experiences. Sometimes it was easier to pass over the world in silence. There was solace, however, in knowing that language was an experience, too, so that experience and language were mutually enriching. It made me want to live well, attentive to what I said and did.

Thinking metaphorically, reflecting on my personal experience of language and of experience itself, meant that metaphor medi-ated my engagement with the world. I could use metaphor to affect the dynamic tension between the world of language and the world of experience, as they spun side by side. Each person who took up a word had a chance to bring experience and language together in a way that had never been done before.

Even though I had so many questions, the interviews with writ-ers were not about answers. No single metaphor would unlock the mystery of what it meant to be creative. There would be no mo-ment when one of the writers said, It's this! and my uncertainty would be resolved. And yet each metaphor renewed the vigour of the question, drawing me deeper. The only way to keep going, to keep living the question, was to find the stories of writing stories. In those accounts of creative experience, a subtle world was made. Formulations of metaphor, A = B, plotted through our conversa-tions, were only hints of the expansive landscape under the surface of our words. What was the feeling of an idea? What was a story? What did it mean to write? The writers' replies gestured with a wel-coming hand to another path between language and the mind.

I had learned this from reading the Brazilian pedagogue Paulo Freire (1921–1997). He described the parallel of *reading the word* and *reading the world.* Literacy was more than being able to define the words in a newspaper. It was about understanding – and challenging – the complexity and the contradictions of one's surroundings. Freire's interest was in economic contradictions, how the oppressed supplied labour and yet still remained oppressed, having internalized the hierarchy that limited their own agency. By reading the world, one could come to know first that one was oppressed, and second, that one was an agent in the making of history –the world was not a fixed state of affairs, but was in a state of constant making. He called this process *conscientizaçao,* or conscientization, coming to awareness. It was the same process that I believed was possible with metaphor. The meaningfulness of words and the world was made together. The way people used metaphor could show not just how those two were connected but how they could be transformed.

A catalogue of metaphors would not be enough. It was too static. Becoming metaphor literate was not a thing to know but a way of knowing. Each metaphor was a single glass surface in a kaleidoscope, supplying light and colour. A survey of metaphors made up the kaleidoscopic view, a composition of dozens of surfaces. Looking at the light was only part of the project. The more important step was to see what happened when metaphors moved – how the light and colour of experience changed when the kaleidoscope of language was turned. Only later would I understand that creativity and metaphor were two sides of the same coin. The problem of how to be creative was another way of asking how one thing could become another.[17]

A = B.

A was the world.

B was one manifestation of the world's possibilities.

With that, my question transformed. *What does it mean to be creative?* had become, *How could the world be otherwise?*

~

Variations on a Survey of
Metaphors for Creativity

Creativity Is Connection

I had done four interviews with writers in Buenos Aires by the time
I met Guillermo Martínez (1962–) in a café in the leafy neighbourhood of Colegiales. I had been introduced to him by a friend who
had written a book about Argentine politics in the works of Julio
Cortázar. Martínez was the author of five novels and dozens of essays and articles. He studied mathematics at Oxford and, partly
because of the commercial success of *Crímines Imperceptibles*, which
was made into a Hollywood film called *The Oxford Crimes*, he was
able to write full time.

Many people had asked him about the connection between
mathematics and literature. The question was usually about the
impact of the former on the latter: How did mathematics inform
the structure of storytelling? Did it lend it a logic, a system? In
Martínez's book of essays, *Borges y la Matemática*, a non-fiction
examination of the mathematics in the fiction of Argentina's
most internationally recognized contemporary literary forefather,
Martínez cited Borges in reference to *la cerradura y la llave*, the
lock and key, of literature and mathematics. I wanted to know if

he thought it could be vice versa: Could literature inform the experience of mathematics? Could the lock become the key?

There is a process of similar creativities in mathematics just as in literature, said Guillermo at our table by the window. What is it that a mathematician looks for? Or how does a mathematician proceed? He or she studies certain patterns, regularities that he or she sees in an ideal world, a world of ideal objects in the Platonic sense. When he finds the cause or the mechanism that makes those objects, he codifies them in a text, which is called a mathematical proof. This has the intention that whoever reads that text can reconstruct that world that he glimpsed, that he managed to decipher, shall we say, at that point.

And what is it that a writer does? Guillermo continued. As a writer, one sees a moment of rupture which gives a new dimension to a story, a story that is, until then, of a slightly liquid medium, without structure, no? And later, by way of coded writing, one gives that story the necessary ligature so that an unprepared reader can follow line by line that text and reconstruct the original world that the writer saw. So, as you can see, the two processes are, from one point of view, similar.

The mathematician with his proof and the writer with his text are both codifiers of something they saw in the first instance, all at once, said Guillermo. It is like when one sees a complete scene, but the language comes successively after it, in the case of the mathematical language as in the literary language. There is a semblance in the creativity.

As Guillermo spoke, I thought of Walter Benjamin's often-cited comment from *The Arcades Project*: "Knowledge comes only in lightning flashes. The text is the

ideas are objects

meaning is a machine, the world is an image, the text is a code

a moment is a surface

a story is a liquid, then a solid

text is a blueprint

long roll of thunder that follows."[1] It seemed that each form of art was that long slow reconstruction of the epiphany when the total idea was glimpsed.

So now, said Guillermo. There's also a very big difference between the language of mathematics and the language of literature, which is that the mathematical language is thought up so that any person reads the same thing in a mathematical text. That also means that it's thought up so that an artificial intelligence, a robot, can check the ligature and in a way corroborate the truth of each of the steps that are elaborated in the proof. That is to say, the language of the mathematician is a language that tries to do away with all possibilities of ambiguity. It's the clearest and most transparent language possible, so that each expression has a univocal meaning.

logic is ligature

truth is a journey

language is a surface

meaning is a voice

Wittgenstein reflected a lot over this, Guillermo added: Until what point can this be achieved? But in principle that's the intention. That whoever reads a mathematical proof always reads the same thing.

Meanwhile the literary language is almost the opposite, Guillermo went on. It's a language that sometimes needs ambiguity. We think, for example, of a suspense novel: the author at once shows and hides in the same phrase, he intentionally looks for certain mistakes, he looks to leave in the semi-darkness a few questions. So on one side it's a language that has a quantity of ambiguities that resonate on distinct planes with the reader, no? Or rather, one tries to transmit some things but in an indirect form, in a form that sometimes is not so clear, because clarity sometimes ends in didacticism in literary language.

knowing is seeing

language is a series of resonating planes

So, from this perspective, literary language does not have clarity as its objective, said Guillermo. Sometimes the objective can even be a certain half-light or experience is a library

a reader is a sponge

darkness. The readers resonate always in different ways with the text because they encounter the text with their libraries, their sensibilities, and their different reading experiences. Two different readers in general absorb the text in very distinct ways.

I was afraid to blink in case I lost a word of what he was saying, even though my tape was recording. The depth of the room divided into two planes, our table where we sat talking and the blur of everything else. I wanted only to stay with his words, that they would keep coming. I didn't consult my notes. They seemed too far away. My mind would spill if I looked at them. It was more important to be completely present, to attend. I was two cupped hands full of water, brimming.

~

I thought of something I had read in a book called *Peripheral Visions* by Mary Catherine Bateson (1939–), writer and daughter of famous anthropologists Margaret Mead and Gregory Bateson. She described witnessing the slaughter of a goat during a religious celebration in Tehran. As she watched, she explained to her young daughter the different parts of the goat's anatomy – that's the heart, those are the lungs– until she realized that she had never seen a goat slaughtered before either. She was extrapolating from what she knew of other animals and of human anatomy but that precise experience had never happened to her, and here she was explaining it as though she recognized it. She reflected that people moved through their lives pairing experiences with words they had heard, not just about anatomy but about emotions and events, like the moment when they recognize, "this is love." The more we experienced, the more places we found for the language of life.

Perhaps it sounds audacious that I was trying to understand the world in Spanish, as if it weren't complicated enough in my first language. But there was a reason. In defamiliarizing language, the labels of an experience were moved around and redefined, resignified and adjusted with each new experience, experience that was otherwise "structured in advance by stereotypes and idealizations, blurred by caricatures and diagrams."[2] There was a liberating naivety in living in a language I had acquired consciously. The history of words was lighter. I attended not only to the content of language but to the experience of language itself. In the encounter with a word or a phrase, I witnessed the transformation of thought into speech and back again. My relationship with language was my most visceral mental experience during that time. Everything around me, inside me, was alive.

Although my second language obscured some truths, it revealed others. Seeing contrast and difference nurtured reflection. For one, there was no such thing as a mundane detail. The most pedestrian exchange emerged into new words. Seeing contrast, similarity, and parallels was integral to making metaphors, too, which relied on finding shared identity between two separate entities. Sure, I would have learned a lot from talking to writers in English, but I might not have noticed the language and experiences I took for granted.

After all, translation wasn't just a practical consideration. It was a philosophical one, too. When the meaning of a word was carried from one language to another, it was transformed. In the transformation, new insight was possible, based partly on the tension between the two identities. The meaning of a concept expanded because it was no longer considered in a singular way.[3]

Later, when I found myself back in Canada, a conversation with a friend would lead to talk about the Chilean-Mexican author Roberto Bolaño.

Are you reading him in Spanish? my friend asked.

Some of it.

Is it different?

I don't know, I said. I'm different in Spanish.

~

Turning to my experience with creative processes, Guillermo continued, Well, various things I see in the long term, no? First, that all my novels were initially short stories. Almost all. Of the five novels I wrote, four arose in the beginning from ideas for short stories. So I consider myself by formation a short-story writer. Almost all Argentine writers initially start as short-story writers. What I imagine before anything, what occurs to me before anything is a certain dramatic situation, and above all the moment that I call the moment of torsion or transition. The point of inflection in which the things that one can see in a certain way for, shall we say, the rule of law of the usual, of the quotidian, can turn so that it is seen in another way in accordance with certain fictional laws that have to do with possibilities for the dramatic, with a certain strangeness of the real, with, in the end, all that can appear in the literary world.

time is a bendable material

familiarity is a breakable law

So that's the moment that I see and also above all the ending, he said, which are two questions that interest me. To assemble a knot of relations, the possibility of seeing things as though there were a kind of prism, and the ending. It's not that the ending necessarily has to be a surprise ending, but it has to give a special density to all that came before. It has to resignify what came before.

turning points and endings are questions, a story is a knot of relations

weight is meaning

And later, he continued, many of the stories as I am writing them start to reveal other potentialities. So for me, to write, the daily exercise of writing, the muscular part, shall we say, has to do with that species of tension that there is between the Platonic idea that we were talking about at the beginning, the initial idea, and the potentialities, the bifurcations, which the practice of writing gives place to.

As one goes along setting things up, said Guillermo, defining the characters, the first movements, there are options that close, roads that close. One realizes that one cannot advance perhaps in all the directions one thought, and meanwhile other options appear.

While Guillermo talked, I thought of another short story by Jorge Luis Borges, "The Garden of Forking Paths." The title didn't only describe the labyrinth laid out by the character who fled his executioner, as I had first thought. There was another meaning: an idea divided in different directions when it was written into a story.

~

I took the subway to Humberto Primo station and walked along a dark street, chased by the echo of my tired shoes. The black trees looked like holes in the wall, wide cracks through which I would not have been surprised to see stars.

Up ahead, a corridor of red light widened from a doorway. Two men stood beside the entrance smoking and talking. One exhaled with his chin tilted up. He looked at me when I passed.

I tried to see into the room beyond, to take in as much as I could without stopping. Across from two women who sold tickets from a high narrow window, a bulletin board was pinned with hundreds of pamphlets. The entrance sloped up into a wide room or a

writing is a body

patio where, in the dim glow, a man and a woman were crouched on a mat. The metal ping of fingers on an aluminum drum pattered through the dark before the doorway drifted behind me and I was alone on the street again.

I kept walking like I was trying to find someplace else. After half a block I checked my phone as an excuse to pivot and returned to the doorway, wishing I could pass beyond it and continue all the way home. But I was looking for someone.

The room smelled of candle wax and stone. The man and woman in the centre were collapsed on one another, back to back, the woman draped over him while he lifted her, his head down. Sitting cross-legged at the edge of the mat was the drummer with an up-turned bowl in his lap, playing rhythms that sounded like an animal running, except that, when he tapped the bowl with a ring that he wore on his finger, it rang like a bell that scared the animal away. There was a small crowd sitting on pillows on the floor, in pairs or in threes, wearing scarves of flickering shadows.

I leaned against the wall beside a curtain where I hoped I would not block anyone's view, where I hoped, in fact, to vanish, my body dissolve so I could watch without being seen. I was suddenly grateful to have this place among strangers, to be with them without changing them. Then, looking around, sadness struck as I envied all of their friendships, seeing that even the ones who were alone had each other, alone together, with a closeness I couldn't match, the only stranger in the room. Standing by the wall was no longer polite, it was cowardly, but the alternative, sitting down next to the nearest couple, a man and a woman who were complete in their beauty together, the candlelight transforming them into a warm, amber fluid – the alternative was too disruptive, even cruel, as if something in myself, not just the room, would have to shatter for me to join them.

I resolved to make eye contact with the next person who passed my post by the curtain. Being seen would herald my arrival. I would be part of the room. But no one came.

On the way out, I asked at the window if they knew Isabel. She was the friend of a friend; she had written to say I could find her there but didn't say when. How strange to look for someone I had never seen before. It usually worked because the force of two people searching brought them together.

She's coming later, said one of the women from the window. Much later, she added.

It was already midnight. For a second my shadow filled the long rectangle of light over the sidewalk as I considered going back inside. The echo of my shoes grew more and more tired as I walked home.

~

Look, said Guillermo. I'm very slow to write. I console myself thinking that there's a time of vigil when one leaves these different possibilities to fight among themselves to see which ones survive and which ones bifurcate.

I wanted to ask him what he does during the vigil. And what is … I began.

This has to do, pardon me, he said, with the fact that I have been a chess player in another epoch, in my infancy.

I understood that from your first novel, *Acerca de Roderer* (Regarding Roderer), I said.

Yes. There is something of the game of chess, too. One has different strategies to carry a novel or a story forward, but many times they meet with options. The waiting time is often necessary for assessing until what point one is inclined toward a certain direction or toward another, until what point to carry a character forward, interrupt them, etcetera.

[margin notes]
writing is a vigil
possibilities are competitors

writing is a game of strategy

Now, what was it you were going to ask me? said Guillermo.

I was going to ask, what do you believe is your role when you are watching these options fight among themselves? Your role is to wait, or to push them ...

Yes, said Guillermo. Then he added: No, no.

What's your relationship to these options then?

It's ... this also occurs in mathematics, he said. In mathematics one often tries different paths, mentally. It's like carrying forward such-and-such hypothesis and it doesn't work and carrying forward the next one and it doesn't work either. One goes along trying different keys, mentally. And a moment arrives when one has tried them all and still the direction that one perceives is the correct one hasn't appeared.

creativity is a scientific method

I thought back to the beginning of our conversation when I had asked Guillermo about the lock and key. I realized that the hypotheses that the writer tested during the act of writing were like a ring of keys that could serve to unlock the secret of the story, as much for the writer as the reader.

creativity is incubation

So there's a moment of waiting, said Guillermo, between waiting and disappointment, when the head keeps thinking but in a more secret way, no? There is a kind of accumulation in which it seems that all the options have been tried but there are a few more, often much more subtle, that one must try, which at first glance don't occur to one. So this time of waiting often has a lot to do with finding a solution that isn't the most obvious, that's a more secret solution, that takes longer to appear.

ideas are objects, visible or invisible

During that time, said Guillermo, one is in the text, one is thinking things, but at the same time one is also listening to what it is that the text has to say, no? Of course, this doesn't have anything to do with the

to write is to listen

mystical or with believing that the text talks by itself, no? Or that it's going to demonstrate itself in a moment. Instead this has to do with being very immersed in the text, so in that moment solutions appear. When they appear, no? because many times they don't appear and one continues on one of these paths that seems better. It's not that all creative moments are like this, but every once in a while one is met with a problem that seems solvable and after a certain time the solution appears.

creativity is seeing

~

It was about to rain when I finally met Isabel at a café near the radio station where she worked. When I had finished stammering through a description of what I was doing in Buenos Aires, she lit a cigarette and looked at me with an expression that said, So what? I realized then that I had no stable centre, that I would doubt whatever she doubted, and that my eagerness to please meant we would never be friends.

We both got up to leave.

There's a park a few blocks away, El Centenario, she said. Let's go for a walk.

Isabel ignored the paths. She chose her own line, going over whatever cement or grass or stones or dirt was on the way, and she touched every tree that she passed.

When she was a little girl, she said, living with her grandmother, there had been no metal bars on the parks, no high fences, and they didn't lock them at night. People used to sit on the grass by the pond under the stars playing music, talking and drinking, but now, things were different. The city was robbing them of everything.

Isabel's voice was tidy and neat in a way I had never heard in Buenos Aires, even though she was born there and had lived there all her life. For one, she pronounced all of her s's. Was it for my benefit that she spoke so clearly? Did she not know how much I wanted to be treated the same as anyone else? But no, it wasn't just for me: later I heard her talk to her friends with the same crisp intonation. It was as though the *porteño* accent had been rubbed away with a coarse grit, leaving the sharp, hard sculpture of her voice underneath.

We walked beside bloated thick-trunked trees called *palos borrachos*, drunken poles. When it started to rain she hooked her arm in mine.

You see? she said, pointing at the thickest tree. This one has had a lot to drink.

What I had thought at first was an indifferent demeanour was something else entirely: it was peace. Her calmness made me less alone.

Too bad you didn't come in summer, she said.

These days I'm more winter than summer.

These days, me too.

On our way back to her office at the radio station, she stopped under an awning to take a phone call. I waited nearby, sitting on a windowsill with my feet dangling in the damp air. For a minute I belonged, then the minute passed.

~

How long should one wait? Guillermo said. In the end one must stop waiting and commit an error. Or rather, elect a solution that you know is not the best but that permits you to continue ahead, no?

How do you know if there is a resolution for your story? I asked.

Well, that's interesting, he said. Look, I, perhaps with my experience as a mathematician, have a sensation that there's also a certain predetermined Platonic form for each fiction that one thinks up. Or rather, one goes along approximating this form, in spite of knowing that one is postulating each phrase oneself, until a moment when one perceives that one is in tune and that things are going well, when the fiction generates as if it were an autonomous mechanism. In a certain way, it generates its own responses and its own solutions.

creativity is completing a shape

writing is tuning
creativity is a machine

And it's not totally absurd to think of it this way, Guillermo added.

I didn't say it was, I laughed.

No, I say it because I think of it from the point of view of the rationalist that I am, because when one formulates laws it's like defining a game from those laws, no? In some ways it's like the story adjusts itself to these initial laws that one postulates at the beginning of the fiction, no? It's curious because sometimes one has the sensation that he really arrived very close to what can be done with the account, yet one sometimes stays with the sensation that another person with a different focus would have written a better story, no? using the same materials.

creativity is a game with rules

completion is a place

Guillermo took a sip of his coffee. He described an essay in which the famous Argentine writer Ricardo Piglia wrote a story as Hemingway would have written it, then wrote the same story as Poe would have written it, then the same story again as Chekhov would have written it.

And then there is a sensation, Guillermo said, once one has read enough, when one says no, I am not going to write this in this way because that is how so-and-so would write it.

Do you believe that there is a "Martinezian" world?

I said, wondering if his own work had become a larger reflection of a singular self.

Well, a big part of my efforts, novel after novel, is to try to do different things, he replied. But yes, one goes along conforming. I always say that the tradition one has to be most careful about is that of one's own books.

Or rather, he added, in writing a book one learns a quantity of things about how to write this book and various similar ones.

I laughed, seeing suddenly that each book was an escape from the one that preceded it. Each work had to flee from its family to make its own family elsewhere, eschewing the safety of patterns.

~

Feliz cumple, I said in the doorway of Isabel's house, the familiar version of happy birthday, passing her two bottles of wine in a plastic bag. She was cleaning up before the others arrived; like a good Canadian, I was the first one there. It was eleven o'clock at night. She preferred to keep busy when people visited – it gave her distance and allowed her to be present without feeling lost.

Her friends arrived. We drank wine and I helped a woman pick seeds out of a plate of marijuana, happy to have something to do, while she talked to a friend who had thirteen cats. I interrupted only once to ask how she named them. One cat was called Gollum. She had found him in a construction site where he had fallen down a hole full of iron shavings. He was grey and black until she brought him home and washed him, when she realized he was white. She said nothing about the other twelve.

The cacophony of the party made it hard to talk. Words slammed into each other or got pulled into the dark. I longed for a meaningful silence. I thought back to the café where I had first met Isabel, between the end of our coffees and the start of her cigarette, when she had told me about a trip to Berlin.

It's one place I could imagine living, she had said, the only place other than here.

Do you take pictures when you travel?

She shook her head.

Me neither. But sometimes I record sounds.

Me, too, she said, showing me how she did it. *Subte en Berlín, dos de noviembre.* Subway in Berlin, second of November.

She said it into an invisible microphone in her hand and then raised it up into the air. At the same time she tilted her head to the side and pulled her ear away from the mic, as if the invisible recorder was as hot and as bright as a torch.

I knew that gesture. It was how I held a microphone when I recorded the ambient sounds of a place, too. Truth was in the way she did it.

Time and silence had collapsed into that one gesture: the moment when she made the recording rushed into the moment at the table at the café in Buenos Aires, where she sat without a microphone but with all the knowledge of how the microphone made her behave. Together those moments came to me in her living room, at her birthday party, days later. I saw in the way she tilted her head that she knew what she was doing, that the microphone had weight and purpose and meaning, and because it was so familiar it was as though she knew my own gestures, too. She had shown me a way of seeing the world and seeing myself. She had done what art did.

At three o'clock in the morning we ran out of Coke and *fernet*, a bitter herbal spirit that I grew increasingly fond of the longer I stayed in Buenos Aires. Isabel and I went to buy more. She hooked her arm in mine as we walked, a habit that made me smile from the inside. There was a queue at the corner store and we waited together without talking, side by side, while a boy behind the counter shouted and passed plastic bags to a man whose car was idling next to the curb with the door open. I felt calm and timeless. There was no need to speak.

We brought the bottles back to the house where I installed myself by the wall with a fragile, reckless joy. I was here, in this new friend's house with her friends and their real lives. I danced in the small crowd, then beamed from the edge of the room, feeling that there was something terrific in being no more than a happy person in a room full of strangers. Isabel came to check on me, not saying anything, just walking over, and I nodded so deeply it could have been a bow. A distinction that was possible in Spanish opened then because of its two verbs for being, *ser* and *estar*, so that the language itself seemed to be saying it: I had always wished to *ser parte*, to be part of a whole in a permanent way that was integral to who I was, while at the same time I was most comfortable when I could *estar afuera*, when I could be outside as a changeable state. I could be part and be apart.

I'm like that, too, said Isabel.

Suddenly the woman with the thirteen cats was collecting dishes from around the room and stacking them next to the sink, where another woman began washing them. A man gathered empty wine bottles with his fingers in the necks and the music ended, opening the dark air to the clink of glass and cutlery. Someone swept. The light from the fridge widened and narrowed. The sky through Isabel's patio door was now a soft aching blue with a line of orange along the lip of the roof where the sun was coming up.

Isabel was asleep in her room. Someone had tucked her in and put a glass of water beside the bed. What good friends! She would wake to a clean home. I touched her arm when I said goodnight. The man who had brought the music saw us to the door and locked it behind us.

I left in a taxi at six o'clock in the morning with three other people who all got out along the way, each of them passing their share of the taxi fare forward until it was too much, letting go of the night like an open hand in the wind, and returned to Constitución as the sun came low through the streets.

~

You said earlier that in fiction, as in mathematics, there is a glimpse of the ideal world. What do you see in this glimpse?

In my case it's as if there were certain points through which the novel is going to pass, as if they were stations, said Guillermo. So I know that a few things are going to happen to the protagonist in his infancy, after that, some other things are going to happen in his youth, and he's going to end in this way. To give you an example, when I was writing *Crímenes Imperceptibles*, I knew how the ending was going to be, I imagined how the two protagonists could find each other, I imagined something of the beginning, how they were going to arrive to the city, but obviously I didn't imagine all the intermediate incidents.

creativity is a journey

What is it that pushes you to do it? I asked. If you already know how it ends, you already know the important steps.

No, said Guillermo. It is still very far from having the necessary internal connection. Or rather, why would he go from here to here? Why would he pass from this station to the other? In other words, it's like having the bones of the structure and it's lacking everything that gives life to the narration.

a plan is a skeleton, a story is a body

But is there something that motivates you to complete it, to make the work, and not leave it without finishing it? I was thinking of how many times I had abandoned projects before they were done, as if they had outrun me and left me behind.

Well, at that early point there is very little, no? said Guillermo. It's very inarticulate. For me what motivates me in all cases is to see all there is in this story. I know that there's going to be this and this and the ending is going to be this. But, well, all that there is in a story for me is what goes in the middle, practically, no? It's the life in each one of the sections. That's the story. It's not the ending that justifies

a story is a shape

everything, nor is it the beginning, no. The life of the story is in all sides.

Then Guillermo's voice hesitated, the only time in our two-hour conversation that he seemed to be searching for words.

It's not exactly … I don't know, in truth, what motivates me … it's odd, no? It's the sensation that I have a story that's worth the shame, that the best I can do is try to write it, this type of …

He trailed off.

I don't need much more motivation than that, he said. I always wrote. I feel sick when I don't write.

~

Dusk fell. Isabel and I sat at a dock in Tigre, north of Buenos Aires, drinking *mate* and eating *alfajores,* hunched over our crossed legs and losing the *yerba* when Isabel spooned it in the breeze. Across the water, a roller coaster wound through the grey light, punctuating our conversation with screams.

I described a day when I had wanted to visit her. After walking toward her house for an hour I realized that I was too sad and tired to talk. At first I thought that visiting her would lift my spirits or that I could simply say, I'm sad and tired, but the closer I got the less I wanted to burden her and instead it became the kind of late afternoon when I needed to let the feeling pass.

I had turned around and walked home. I took a longer way, from Palermo to Corrientes, which I liked so much, especially the part where the bookstores and the trees began, and then down Callao and finally Entre Ríos. I knew all the stores after the intersection with Belgrano, all the breaks in the sidewalk stones, at least I thought I did, or I recognized them when I saw them, and I greeted the butcher on the corner before turning onto Solís. The house had been empty, which had been a relief.

What a strange idea of friendship you have if you think that would be a burden, said Isabel.

I told her about walking home from my tango lesson one night, too, which made Isabel laugh because I was another tourist learning tango. I had looked up at the lights on Avenida 9 de Julio, the widest avenue in the world, thinking that the city wasn't finished with me and that I wasn't finished with the city. Even though I was tired and wanted to rest, wanted to go home, another part was squaring with all the things that the city could be. The night sang something so rhythmic it was more like a chant, not a challenge but a ceremony. I knew, I told her, gesturing across the water toward the amusement park, that the taxi drivers and the booksellers and the café waiters had no idea what it meant to me to be here and to want to come back. I needed to come back, or at least to say that I would, to console myself in that moment of nostalgia, loneliness, and wanting to belong.

Then, because of the way Isabel looked at me, I told her about a time years before when I had lost hold of everything and fell apart from the inside, like my organs were chunks of ice that broke off and tumbled into black water. I had done things then that I still couldn't explain, didn't know how to explain, which is when I discovered dancing, that thing beyond language and reason and how, in a way, it had saved me.

And how is it now? she asked. We had packed up the *mate* and the bag of *alfajor* crumbs and were walking back toward the train.

Like another person, I said, as if it happened to someone else who has taken the time to teach me what he learned.

But in Canada I still think about it, I continued, as though dying is on the underside of leaves or in the noise that a fly makes, and I assume it's just around the corner whether by illness or by accident. I can hear a voice that must be my voice although it's longer, not higher or lower, just longer, stretching from one side of death to the other and passing through this bright light in the middle that is the shock of my life. It's the voice that declares itself when I imagine meeting death, and the voice pleads: there is still so much I wanted to do.

The words were coming easily and Isabel was looking at me as if this made sense. The train back to Buenos Aires arrived and emptied. A sea of people crushed toward the open doors, running.

I told her that when I travelled it was different. When I travelled I was immersed in being alive. I could even feel the possibility of dying in a way that was vibrant and vivacious like a crazy adventure that made everything sacred. But in stillness, at home, dying came as anxiety.

She reached back and took my hand as we ran across the platform, breathing when the train doors closed. The station pulled away and blurred into blocks of graffiti at the back of grey cement houses.

We sat on wooden stools in her living room and opened a bottle of wine. It was midnight. I described a short story I had read by Robert Walser about a man who got throat cancer. One day it was difficult to swallow, then more difficult with each day until he was drinking soup through a straw and his face was gaunt. His wife and kids watched him wither. They must have known where this was headed. He died two months later. That's me, I thought when I read it. That's what will happen. If not my throat then something else. No matter when it came it would be too soon. I would not find peace. I would leave people as they said goodbye, I would leave them before I died. I would seek comfort inside myself, shutting people out although they would never know it. I would keep up appearances but every last meeting would just make it harder. I had to hurry. There was so little time. I hadn't done what I set out to do. Any minute now it would hurt to swallow. But the next day all I had done was go for a walk and read a book, a different book, in a sunny café window, stopping sometimes to look at a bird that pecked at seeds on the sidewalk.

We opened a second bottle of wine and ordered *empanadas* over the phone from a bakery that delivered. By now the door to language was wide open. Words came from a place beyond me, a history of sound tumbling from my mouth. They picked up traces of my life on their way past, like flocks of tiny bats leaving a cave with darkness on their wings. Shapes came streaming. My lips and my tongue were not making the words, they were moving around them. The sounds had their own momentum. My work was to hold the space, to concentrate just enough so that words could fly. They stopped moving if I thought of them directly. The flow faltered. My mouth and my tongue, expecting momentum, closed and tripped – a bat slammed against the wall of the cave. But if I stayed open and loose, giving in to lucidity that was also madness, language remade the world through a hole in my head, my little body transformed into a passage for possibilities so strange and gorgeous I swooned, holding the space for the flight of a sentence.

The wine and the food were finished. Isabel and I took turns smoking. The city didn't need us. Then, her face calm, stopping sometimes to brush an ant from the table, Isabel told me more about her life than I had told her about mine. I put my hand on her hand and kept it there until it got sweaty. If one of us was going to cry it would be me. We laughed like something was breaking. The sun came up. She pulled out the cot in her storage room and gave me some blankets. I lay still in the early morning, listening to the chirp of a new winter bird outside.

~

Would you say that what you are doing is creative? I asked. Do you use that word?

Yes, of course, said Guillermo.

The word doesn't bother you.

To the contrary. I'm a defender of the idea of originality. To be creative is to achieve something that in some point hasn't been done before. A creative person for me is essentially a person who can find a new angle, a new form of seeing the world, a new form of

creativity is perspective

writing some things. Italo Calvino also has a very interesting essay that's called "Mundo escrito y mundo
no escrito" (The written world and the unwritten

to write is to widen the
world

world). Part of creativity for me is to widen a world
that hasn't been written. To find a way to tell what has-
n't been told. But also to tell it in a different form and
with a different angle from what has been told. So creativity can be in distinct aspects of literature but for
me it's the number one attribute that I use to judge a
literary text.

To play a text? I had heard *jugar*, "to play," when he
said *juzgar*, "to judge."

To judge, Guillermo said flatly.

Pardon me.

When I read as a reader, Guillermo continued, I
have to have the feeling that the writer in front of me
is creative, is profound, is intelligent. There are various questions, no? But the first is the question of creativity, which one perceives immediately. Or rather, if

creativity is surprise

I see that it's more of the same, if you know that you've
seen it before … this plays a lot with the question of
reading, of the reader just as much as of the writer.
The more reading one has done the more it costs to
be surprised. But one perceives immediately at once

creativity is weight

where there is a certain literary density, no?

a turn is contact

It's curious, this experience, said Guillermo. The
turn has touched me to be a judge in different literary
competitions with other writers who are very dissim-
ilar in terms of their literary preferences, but when

moments are
movements

the moment arrives to say of the hundred works presented which are the four or five best ones, we all co-
incide on the same ones. We can differ after, if we give
the first position to this or this or this, but there are
always four or five works out of every hundred, no?

Four or five out of a hundred that emerge on their own, that shine by themselves, that you immediately recognize, here is a writer. You realize because of a quantity of errors they avoid and because of questions they present with a certain ability, that this person knows what they are doing, that they have read, that they avoid such-and-such error and in exchange they achieve such-and-such things. It is something impressive in that sense.

mediocrity is a container
creativity is luminescence

~

That week there was a story in the news about a man who was parking his car in his garage when two thieves dashed under the gate before it closed. The man shot and killed one of the thieves; the other thief shot and killed the man. Journalists speculated that he had been trying to protect his wife and kids, who were awakened by the sound of gunshots as the man came home for the last time.

Also in the news was a teenager in the suburb of San Martín who had been attacked after school. A group of boys pushed him until he fell and kicked him until he died. The thieves, who had become killers, escaped with his mobile phone. The event was recorded by a security camera outside an electronics store. The footage showed grainy stills of black and white ghosts lurching toward a fixed point before vanishing and starting again. Both stories were discussed by evening TV hosts who looked relieved to have a break from chronicling the country's latest slide into economic crisis.

But the news that bewildered me most was a sign taped to the wall of the Castro Barros subway station that read: "On March 2nd at 1500h Alejandro Ferrer, age 23, was stabbed and killed here; if you saw anything please contact this number, he could have been your brother or your son or your friend so don't be passive." It included a photograph of a young man with brawny arms and a thin beard, smiling in the sun.

On this very platform? I wondered. In the middle of the afternoon? I checked the time, absurdly relieved to discover that it was five o'clock and not three.

Later, a friend's mother told me to always be careful on the streets and in theatres but especially in the subway, to carry as little money as possible and always in your front pocket, to look down, don't talk to anyone, just get where you are going because there are thieves, thieves everywhere, especially if they know you are foreign. Another woman remembered wistfully that it wasn't always like that. When she was young she walked home in a miniskirt at any time of the night, but that was before the drugs came. Now taxis were dangerous, too. They could take you anywhere.

A blanket of anxiety stretched over Buenos Aires, a feeling that crime not just could but would happen at any moment. People were braced for it, so that stories on the news only strengthened their suspicion, anticipation, and fear. Accounts of crime offered a place to unload the feeling of not knowing where or when it would happen next.

Guidebooks and gossip said that Constitución, the neighbourhood where I was staying, was rough. The train station four blocks away was infamous for stabbings, theft, and drugs. I took secret pride in telling people where I lived, as though it licensed me to know something that was true and real about the city. By the time I left, I was fond of Constitución, grateful that I hadn't stayed in Recoleta, Belgrano, or Palermo – hip, chic, and elegant neighbourhoods of comfort and wealth. But the first time I asked Eugenio if I should be concerned when coming home at night he looked at me like I was an idiot. Exasperated, he flicked his hands in the air.

It's safe! It's safe, okay?

A few weeks later I considered a trip to San Martín for an interview, a trip that others were cautious to endorse without the usual advice – carry nothing more than what you need, come back before dark, know exactly where you are going – and I asked Eugenio again, having forgotten his first reaction. This time he stamped his foot and made a noise as if he was spitting on the floor.

It's safe, okay?! Nothing will happen!

He stormed into the other room to gurgle a *mate* and read on the computer. Then I remembered: Eugenio had lived through two dictatorships. He had fled to Brazil with his family. He had come back and lived under a pseudonym. He was the editor of a national Marxist newspaper that chronicled the unjust treatment of the poor. He had seen enough to know what real violence was.

During our regular visits at cafés around the city, Gloria and I agreed there was something sensational about Buenos Aires's fascination with crime. Where was it? we wondered, having seen so little of it ourselves. Surely there was no more or less of it than in any city of so many millions of people. Life in Buenos Aires teetered on the blade of a knife, balanced, for now, always with the chance of falling, always with the chance of scars.

~

Do you believe that creativity can be taught?

Not exactly that the creative part can be taught, said Guillermo, but yes, one can teach oneself a quantity of errors that one shouldn't commit. And yes, one can stimulate oneself to find, for example, different paths to respond to the question. One can attempt exercises of this type. There are variations of the same story. Look, in *A Thousand and One Nights* it appears like this, in Chinese traditions it appears like this, in Argentine literature it was done this way … to follow what is called the forms of fiction. Something like what Piglia did, or what Borges does many times.

Part of the oeuvre of Borges is that, Guillermo con-

history is a shape tinued. To trace a class of fictional problematic in distinct cultures and then develop his own example. I believe that one can give exercises to kids something of that style. Look how this story is like this, like that. After reading four, five stories that are more or less similar in their essentials, now think of a variant that's not any of these, that's personal. So there's an exercise

creativity is a variation in creativity with respect to tradition, no?
on the past

I call that creativity, said Guillermo. It's not the new for the sake of the new. Instead it's the new that confronts a quantity of things that have already been done. The new has to struggle in intensity, in profundity, in subtlety with all that has been done behind it.

As Guillermo talked, I imagined my attempts at creativity facing a wall of better work, the dozens of works I knew and the thousands I had never heard of, so that all my projects were obliterated by the indomitable crush of history. When would I know enough?

Something in my focus waned. I would stay as long as Guillermo let me, until he gave me a sign – a look over my shoulder, or if he leaned back with both hands on the table, elbows locked, ready to push off; or something even quieter, a tired sigh that came through his eyes when the rest of the day, the things to do next, started to take shape in his face. I would vanish the instant I detected boredom. Until then, I dug for caffeine in my body, hearing myself an hour from now calling back to keep going, stay present, this will only happen once.

That demands a profound consciousness of what already exists, I said.

Clearly, said Guillermo. Like a foundation. That's how science is done. Or rather, what's creativity in the sciences? It's to find the solution to a problem. But on top of that it's to maintain all the anterior responses. One can't contradict the anterior. The new theory of physics has to explain a phenomenon that hasn't been explained, and conserve all the anterior explanations. There's something of that in the creativity of literature, too.

Every person has a life to tell, Guillermo said without prompt. That life will usually be their own. It will serve them once. If he or she had a life full of adventures maybe he or she can take two or three novels from that, but they can't go further than themselves. This's how it seems to me.

Absently he lifted his spoon from beside the empty coffee cup and put it back down. The tiny silver clattered. The interview was coming to an end.

There are two main sources in the history of literature, don't you agree? he said. Literature, and one's own life, or the life to which one has access, which may belong to family, friends, etcetera. To me it seems that creativity passes a little beyond all of this, beyond the immediate, beyond a chronicle of one's self.

Unless, Guillermo added, what one has to say is said in a form that hasn't been said, no?[4]

creativity is accumulation

the self is a territory

creativity is transcendence

~

On the sidewalk in front of the café, I thanked Guillermo again and again. When he was out of sight I leapt in the air and my face broke with a smile. I covered my mouth with my hand, then gave up and beamed at the street, which blurred and swirled. Our conversation was a jittery explosion of hope, carrying me forward, lifting me up. His words had been spoken to me! Little me!

Then I hesitated. Did my path avoid errors or was it

built on them? Had I considered the ways the same moment had been handled in history? Having weighed each possibility, had I responded in a manner that was personal and true to myself? Did I, let alone my work, have any density at all?

I went to kick a pebble that was balanced on the edge of the sidewalk and missed. At that moment four kids darted from the store next to me. The skin on my neck tingled.

Give it back, give it back, said a woman, her voice lifting like a question, then, when she said it twice again, falling hard into each word as though she were hitting the kids with the sounds.

A girl who was wearing a red sweatshirt and couldn't have been more than twelve years old turned to look back over her shoulder just as the woman broke into a run. For a second it looked as if the girl were laughing. She dropped a handful of scarves on the sidewalk. The four kids spread into the busy intersection, one crossing the avenue and another crossing the street, with the girl in the red sweatshirt and a taller boy in black turning down the road to the side while the woman scooped up the scarves behind them. She sprinted back to the entrance of the shop and threw the scarves in the doorway, shouting that they had to call the police, and kept running past the door as if to catch the kids on the other side of the block. The owner of the store next to her nodded blankly under her awning but didn't move. People continued to walk past.

At the end of the block, I saw in the distance the girl in the red sweatshirt, paused as though she were waiting for a signal that would send her left or right. She grinned, then vanished around the corner.

I gripped my recorder. The threat of being robbed meant more after an interview than before. I was carrying something irreplaceable, a string of words hung across the time of our meeting, hard bits of air that were suspended like a song that no one else had heard yet. But I felt a breezy excitement, too, as though I were the girl in the red sweatshirt and we both had escaped with something that we wanted, something that held great value as much for the way we had obtained it as for what it was. I was relieved to witness finally a microcosm of the larger fear. It was a safe way to watch the anxieties of property play out. If I was afraid, it was for the world that would be created by children who stole for fun. Children who laughed when they sprinted away from damage. Children who, in a few years, could kick a boy to death for his phone. Surely the city was failing.

But Buenos Aires was always failing. The best of it was in a past that animated the present with melancholy and a vain hope for a wayward return to a home that no longer existed. The city staggered through time like Walter Benjamin's angel of history with its back to the future, except that the angel of Buenos Aires was singing with one hand clutching its chest. Against all odds, new things still happened in a hundred years of nostalgia. In a place that talked so much about its broken rules, it was mundane to see that crime was this simple. It was popular, as in of-the-people, these were children, even children playing, a fact that disturbed me only when I considered all children playing like this at once. Instead, for this one moment of one day, it was weirdly logical. Of course, I would feel different when it finally happened to me.

~

Creativity Is a Conversation

Mariana Docampo and I met for our interview in a café across from Parque Saavedra. She too was a connection from the friend who had written about Cortázar and politics. While Mariana talked, I listened with the hands of my mind outstretched to catch her speech so that I could bring parts of it back to her, saying, look what I found in your words, what do you think? Two hours vanished into minutes.

In one of Mariana's stories in a collection called *La fe: Relatos* (The Faith: Relatings), the narrator remarked, "Comprendí en ese momento que las palabras eran un límite para la comunicación entre las especias"[5] (I comprehended in that moment that words were a limit for the communication between species).

I wondered, wasn't that limit between people, too, not just between species?

Did I write "species"? or "people"? Mariana said, surprised. Well, yes, I believe so. I believe that the language for expressing one's self is very precarious. It's the only thing we have. Well no. It's not the only thing. We have other manners, we have gestures, we have other things. We don't only have words. It's one of the modes, not even the most efficient mode, for me to make you understand.

She paused as if to catch up to herself.

I think a lot in relation to language, she continued, and in general in what I write there's a lot of reflection on language and on the limits of language. In principle, it's one plane of the universe and of social relations. We communicate with what we can and we have certain conventions. But I believe that it all could be something else. That everything could be interpreted absolutely in another manner.

For example, she said, it happens in discussions with one's partner. Someone says something, but the language is very limited. I say this, the other person says otherwise, and in reality one has to account for thousands of other variables that surround what's being said to be able to understand it. One has to be thinking of much more than only what is said. So, yes, for me language is a limit.

Stories – Mariana preferred the word *relatos*, like relatings, accounts – are doubts, she said. What interests me is to put in question what's said. That in some moment the reader distrusts all that one is saying in the relating.

If you watch television, Mariana continued, if you watch TN and you watch Canal 7, for example, which are the two poles, it's very clear that Argentine reality is a construction. A family that watches TN will have one reality and a family that watches Canal 7 will have another. Without a doubt neither one of them is the reality.

But the theme, she said, is that one who is raised in either reality, when he or she soon sees something else, everything collapses. The point is not to go to the other side as if it were the true reality. That's why I always try to make everything that's constructed deconstruct itself as a mode of advancing. Distrust everything. Don't keep yourself in fixed blocks. Instead maintain permanent movement in order not to fall in the trap of lies. It's a little of that.

ideas are structures, knowledge is a journey convention is a box

It interests me to work precisely with that when I write, she shrugged. To deceive the reader with a reality that could be otherwise. That the reader comes in to the writing and after, show them that all this could become something else.

And it seems to me, I said, thinking of the ephemeral, ambient quality of Mariana's prose, that you are working that by way of the voice, the narrative voice. More than the plot or the events, it's the narrator. Their attitude, their personality.

Clearly, she said. In this book I do that more specifically. The narration was one of the things I was interested in working with. For example, in "La Raíz" ("The Root," one of the stories in the collection *La Fe*), one doesn't understand much about who is narrating. I wanted it to be a voice that one distrusts at some moment. What interests me is precisely to assemble that tension, to enter the fiction but at the same time to have something that moves you away from it to be able to reflect on it.

creativity is an assemblage of tensions

It seems to me that is what happens in general with life, she added. I enter it from one side and suddenly I encounter something that changes it.

That moment interests me, I said. When you look around and realize that life has changed.

language is a
community

knowledge is a shape

knowledge is a path

Yes, said Mariana, that everything could be otherwise. A little like science fiction. You are bred into a
discourse where all things have their place. What happens if all that does a turn and becomes something
else? All that you were acquiring, the language, the
forms to understand things, what happens if all that
does a turn? In my personal experience, there was a
moment when everything turned and for me this transition is devastating. Because it's like returning to be
born again.

~

Avenida 9 de Julio, the so-called widest avenue in the
world, had twenty lanes and ran north-south down the
east side of the city. The pedestrian crossings were divided by large cement islands where, during the day,
people paused and waited for the next light so they
could cross at a leisurely pace. But it was midnight.
And the signal had changed to walk.

I looked up in a rare moment when I could see the
night sky. Billboards, buildings, even the obelisk itself
were reduced to marginal, insignificant chatter at the
sides of a deep silence. When I looked down, the signal was already blinking and I was only halfway across
the expanse.

Three men loomed up ahead on the cement island,
surrounded by traffic, wiping their squeegees in a
bucket of dark water. I arrived just as pairs of lights
rushed by on either side, sealing us together.

I clenched my teeth and fixed my eyes on the farther shore.

The tallest of the men lumbered at me with his
squeegee raised. His body was full of shadows, except
for his eyes, which had the streaks of white lights pass-

ing furiously across them. My stomach was a knot. I didn't know what to do with my hands. I had time to wonder if this was when everything would change.

Give me money, the man snarled.

When he blinked the city blinked with him, closing and opening the darkness.

If I took out my wallet to give him money, it would be the end. Why hadn't I put extra bills in my front pocket as I had done every other day, anyplace where I could pass it to him in one clean stroke without rummaging around in my jacket? Things went wrong when I stopped paying attention.

So this was why I had seen the stretch of another man's stride on a different night as he crossed the same avenue, his long legs and the bend in his elbow, dashing across all the lanes at once. The charcoal drawing in la Boca had foreseen it, too, the figure lunging across the page into the night.

It was impossible to run. Traffic ravaged both sides of the ce-ment island at a hundred kilometres an hour. This man would strike me down on a stage that a thousand cars would see, each one passing their headlights over the scene of a stranger crushing another stranger, none of them getting more than a glimpse before the avenue swept them along. By the time one of them called the police, the damage would be done. What would they find? Surely not my hope, my memories, my love.

An entire city of my experience had converged on this spot, so that none of the things I had done that day or that year, none of the feelings I had shared or conversations I had had, would have any bearing on what happened next. If he wanted to hurt me there would be no assessment of my merit. He would not check to see how much my parents cared. I was a possibility without a name be-tween the pause of windshields in traffic.

I looked into his eyes. I tried to convey a wide sense of peace, of openness, not defying him but lifting myself up in self-assurance and goodwill. He was tired, even disappointed. I wanted to help him even though he could destroy me. My survival depended on him. Did he not know that all he had to do was grab me by my jacket with his fist scrunched under my chin, lift me up and bring his face closer, and he would have it all? Of course, he knew.

Disculpa, I said gently. Forgive me.

He mumbled something I couldn't understand and stepped forward. Still looking into his eyes, I said *disculpa* again. I was mystified that language had kept me safe this long, that words had protected my body.

Pain bent across his eyes without changing the rest of his expression. I thought of a cold metal pipe falling through the night air, never landing. Pain turned to anger. His eyes hardened.

Disculpa, he sneered with teeth.

Then, like a whisper over his shoulder, the traffic light changed from green to red. The walk signal lit up on the distant shore. The other two men ran between the cars, waving squeegees. The one who had been facing me blinked, the city closed, then opened, and he lumbered after them.

~

You are a writer but you also dance tango, I said. Tell me about creativity in tango.

I do Queer Tango, Mariana explained. I'm clarifying it for you because traditional tango has other manners of creativity. There are very defined roles in tango, the person who leads and the person who is led. In traditional tango it's the man who leads and the woman who is led. In Queer Tango they're not fixed roles. That is to say, either identity can occupy them. The role of guiding, traditionally the role of the man, is the one who has the possibility of creating figures. In tango you are all the time improvising. You don't have a structure that you have to repeat ... pardon me, yes there are structures, but there's no choreography. It's a dance of improvisation. There are certain movements that are of the tango. You have to do certain basic steps. And above this formula you are able to create. Meanwhile, the woman, or the role of the guided, inside the possibilities that are given by the one who guides, can make what are called "adornments." Which is to move the feet in a way, make a flourish, et cetera. When you do Queer Tango both people have to be very prepared for guiding or being guided. It seems to me that the creativity is given in the improvisation.

In traditional tango, Mariana continued, creativity has to do with the space that the man gives to the woman and in that space the woman can be creative. What you have in Queer Tango is the possibility that in any moment it can become something else.

It's not total abandonment, she clarified. You have a structure and once you learn it, you articulate it and go along creating.

creativity is elaboration within a zone

So for you, I asked, can you use tango to understand what passes in writing? To have this tradition or this system that already exists and later put something creative?

I'll give you an example, I just thought of it now, said Mariana. I think there's a difference. That formula, that scheme that there is in the tango, is a site. In writing, no. No, it's more vast what happens in writing. I look for a site when I write. I try to work with things, with the Internet … I look for a scheme and I work on that. I like to always have something so that I don't lose myself completely. In writing, one assembles as one goes. In tango you already have it. It's a convention. And that makes it also a site. It's not so vast.

writing is a place

writing is a structure

~

A helicopter circled over the president's office at the Casa Rosada, although not the kind for taking the president's children to school. Avenida de Mayo was closed to traffic because of protests, but the occasional van with the logo of a TV station zoomed past, lifting a swirl of paper fliers behind it. A man packed up a camera and folded a tripod before walking across the grass. Two other men drank from a clear-plastic water bottle under a tree. Otherwise the plaza was empty.

Earlier that day, Avenida Callao north of Rivadavia was blocked by labour groups beating drums and carrying green banners. They came from across the country, some travelling for hours and even days, moving in loud clumps through the centre of the city to converge on the government buildings. The tall stone offices that flanked Callao amplified the drums and stirred the noises together. Firecrackers pierced the air with a dry bright snap and left a second of stillness in their wake.

A member of the president's party had threatened a national transport strike in opposition to the president's decision not to raise truck drivers' wages. The party member had been a truck driver himself at one time. The demonstration was to show what it would be like to have no trucks, no shipments of goods coming in or out of the city, no transport. There was no traffic. There was no fuel.

It seemed as if every weekend waves of protest passed by the windows of cafés where I wrote and read. For a few minutes drums and banners were everywhere, fluttering against the glass like butterflies, and from the strained throats of men and women came chants about the world they wanted to live in, not this world but one within reach. It wasn't long ago that the same thing could have gotten them killed or disappeared. I remembered an Argentine film I had seen, *Noche de los Lápices* (Night of the Pencils), based on the true story of seven teenagers who were kidnapped by the military government for protesting increased bus fares in 1976. They were tortured. Six of them were killed. The seventh escaped to tell the story. It had been the fate of thousands. These voices rose in similar formations, different people with the same courage to make noise against the silence.

How would I join them? How would I participate in the history of the world that I wanted?

I was too frightened of loud noises to shout, too gentle to throw a firecracker. I needed a quieter way.

~

In both cases, in literature and in dance, you talk about the feeling of connection, I said. Is that connection something that you use to understand what is creativity?

Yes, said Mariana. Because if not, it's impossible. If you're not connected to what you're making, it can't be. In tango there's something physical, you connect or you repel. You are present [*estás*] or you are not present [*no estás*]. You have to find yourself, to be in you, to relate yourself to the other. With writing it's more complicated because there's no physical distance between you and the work. You are with the computer, you are with your head. It's a little crazy what passes. The physical instance of writing is like a non-body.

creativity is presence

writing is a non-body

If feeling yourself connected is the part of writing that enchants you, what is it that disconnects you from writing? I asked. Is there something that doesn't please you, that frustrates you?

The difficult part is the quantity of hours in a crazy state, she said. At times I pass all of a day writing and you disconnect yourself also from yourself.

Mariana said she tried not writing, thinking that she could just dedicate herself to tango and that would be enough. But it caused her anguish. She missed talking about profound themes.

Maybe in the future, she said, I could just do tango and be more human. Connect myself more with my

writing is connection

house, with my plants. I don't have that. That complicates me. I would like to be in connection with what surrounds me and not so much in my head. That's what complicates me the most.

~

I met Abasi twice, but everything that mattered between us happened in the last minute before we said goodbye.

She was from Cairo, by way of Princeton, and was in Buenos Aires for a short course on Argentine literature. Introduced by the friend of a friend, we met at the obelisk and spent the afternoon wandering the Museo Latinoamericano de Bellas Artes in Recoleta, moving separately through small rooms where carved wooden trunks and hammered plates of silver slumped in the shadows of glass cases. It was a Thursday and by chance the museum tickets were free that day, which made me feel as if we had won a prize, that we were on the inside of the city. There was something competitive about that first meeting, both of us insisting on speaking in Spanish, comparing what we had learned of Buenos Aires, probing what the other had found that could be shared.

Abasi was fanatical about Peru. She had lived there for a year. It had the most delicious food and the most interesting history and the best people. It might have been because I had lived in Chile that I was defensive. But there was one moment after we left the museum and walked in the cold grey streets for an hour under a bitter wind, one moment that was a glimpse of what would happen the second and only other time I would see her. We stepped into a café to warm up and talked about the South African author J.M. Coetzee. She had read one of his books a long time ago and had been meaning to read his others. I brightened, wanting to give myself to her, caring, excited for what she would find in books that had inspired me so much.

Weeks passed. Three days before her flight to Cairo we met again at the obelisk. We tucked ourselves into a table by the window in a café on Avenida de Mayo where Julio Cortázar had written *Los Premios* (*The Winners*), his first published novel although not the first novel he wrote. This time I was touched that we insisted on Spanish, the pride of new language having settled, and we had spent enough time in the city to find a more secure version of ourselves. There was less to prove. Meeting in our acquired language was an act of respect for where we were, like hanging one's hat while indoors.

There was still a great distance between us for the first two hours of our talk. We traded observations about the city, what we had found, where we had been, how our projects were going – her classes, my interviews. Then something changed. Maybe it was because we had been sitting there so long or because it had started to rain or because she was leaving and I would be leaving, too, knowing that we were in this together although in different times for different reasons and living in different bodies with different plans for each of us. I was no longer relating facts of my history or repeating lines I had heard myself say. We were sharing in a present moment, in the questions that we were living right then. It was the only way of truly meeting someone.

We had been talking about Paris in the 1920s and how foreigners could live there in relative luxury as long as their money came from elsewhere. One could write in cafés and meet other writers in a city that was falling apart and being rewritten and maybe, just maybe, it had felt then as it did now to be in Buenos Aires.

Could you come back to live here? Abasi asked.

Something in the way she said it, or the way she squinted as she waited to hear what I would say, made me feel as though there were no better time to tell her all the things I didn't know. For there was a difference between dreaming of this place and the reality of actually finding an apartment, paying bills, trying to make community. We both knew it was complicated to belong in Buenos Aires as an outsider. It was complicated to belong in Vancouver or in Cairo, too, belonging anywhere.

I don't have roots in any city anymore, said Abasi, but it bothers me less and less. That's what frightens me.

When I can't find my roots, I build a home with leaves, I said.

She smiled. That's a good metaphor.

We got up to go. Abasi stopped.

What's the secret to partnership? She asked. Do you find someone who lives where you've found yourself or do you go there with someone?

I don't know, I said, suddenly sad. I think more of places, places I want to go, and I go there.

I walked alone to San Telmo for a tango class, thinking about how different it had been to meet Abasi as an event and then to meet her honestly. In the first one, when meeting was just an event, we were acquaintances whose lives bumped against one another but still remained separate. There were a lot of events in my Buenos Aires. Our second visit had started as an event but it transformed into the other kind of meeting, the kind that was an honest encounter, much rarer because we became ourselves through one another.

I hurried to San Telmo, late for class, while the thought of Abasi became bright and new. I wanted to call her and see her again before she left on Saturday, to go quietly crazy for three days together until the city used up all our secrets. But we never met again.

~

Talking about your process of writing, I said, does it cost you? Or does it come to you with fluidity?

The problem is between terminating one thing and grabbing another, said Mariana. When I'm writing it flows more. I start with twenty distinct things and if I don't go to any of them, I'm in anguish. When I am already in something, it's more facile. Writing is a network that I go along assembling with words. Once I have that, I find what I wrote and even if I'm not con-

creativity is a web of relations

nected with the story, I go along correcting words, repetitions. Then, in a moment I hook myself and go on writing. It's beautiful because it's work in which I don't have to be thinking what happens next. As if it were a frame that already exists and you go along correcting it. I go out, I read, I play with the Internet, with books. It seems to me that it's like the construction of a site from which I can go out, and to which I can return.

inspiration is a hook

creativity is a place

And this network isn't only in the leaf that you are writing, I said, savouring that the word for page, *hoja*, was the same as the word for the things that grew on trees, *hojas*, as if they had traded places and I could see letters written on plants and pages fluttering in the branches. But also in the act of writing itself, no?

Mariana nodded gravely. It is as if it were a loom to which I go and give a little stitch. She plucked an invisible thread in the air. The site is also rooted in the materiality of the words. It's something that the material already has, when it's open. Writing is a network, but it's also a state. The problem is when it's not open.

creativity is a textile

language is a material

creativity is a container

My mind trembled as if it had just come out of a river into the sun. The joy of our talk was showing plainly in my eyes.

What is it that makes this network open or closed? I asked hopefully.

Magic! she laughed. I don't know how it's achieved.

My heart sank, knowing that I would never know either. What do you do when you feel that something has closed?

I wait, she said. I occupy myself with getting my other books moving, I dance tango, I try to get money, I read or prepare workshops. I occupy the time with other things. It's difficult because you don't know when it's really open. At times you open various things and none of them are conducive. Or they are preparatory for something else.

But every little while, she added, I come back to see if it functions or not.

~

Gloria invited me to a barbecue. We stood on a rooftop drinking wine from plastic cups, keeping warm beside the carbon, turning our heads when the wind blew smoke in our eyes. I met a painter. I showed him pictures on my phone of charcoal portraits I had done in Canada and talked about the drawing classes as though I still went to them once a week.

I want to learn how to draw, I told him, hoping to cultivate the eagerness and naivety that made room for people to teach me things.

The painter was unmoved.

It seems like you already know how to draw, he said. What's left is to do something with that.

~

Do you believe one can learn to be creative? I asked.

I don't know if learned, but exercised, yes, said Mariana. To learn implies something that one doesn't have, that's exterior. I don't believe there's anybody that doesn't have creativity. Perhaps not incentivized or exercised, but it's there.

She gave me an example.

Let's say you are Adrián now, but you could continue to be the Adrián of 2010. It seems to me that one changes naturally, but there are people that don't change, and it seems to me that to change is also an exercise. Like writing. If I don't make a physical movement toward my computer and sit down to write, I don't

write. If you don't exercise creativity, you watch tele- creativity is resistance,
vision and it kills you. The opposing energy is very creativity is survival
strong.

I believe there are quite a lot of possibilities for
creativity in Argentina, Mariana continued. I was in
Europe giving tango classes and I realized that the
artistic question is more complicated there. Those
who already have their place are able to make art, but
in general it costs a lot more to be creative. Here we
talk, then we say, what are we going to do now? Are
we going to take another coffee somewhere else? It
seems to me that it doesn't happen in other places so
naturally. Here one thing leads to another and you creativity is a sequence
connect yourself with each other. This seems like a of connections
creative life to me also.

I don't know how it would be in Canada, she said.
But I remember in Switzerland you have to do things
with three weeks of anticipation and in three weeks I
was leaving so nobody was prepared to sit down for a
coffee. A lot of solitude. And what can that produce?
The majority of people who live like that are bitter,
sad, alone, but when there's more movement it seems
to me that there's more place to exercise creativity.

She paused. I am a chatterbox, no?

I beamed, cheering with my eyes. How often had I
been frustrated and alone in Vancouver because everything seemed to be organized weeks in advance. I
longed for the kinds of possibilities she described.
Maybe that was why I was open to Buenos Aires – because Buenos Aires was open to me.

~

I ran into Claudia from the bakery in front of a printing shop in the neighbourhood of San Cristóbal. The city, like its stories, was made of intersecting lines.

The feeling of knowing her arrived before I remembered her name or where we had met, even before I knew who she was. Her upturned eyes, magnified by her glasses, wobbled between strangers on the sidewalk. Something leaned forward – not her, because I still didn't know where the feeling was coming from, just a bending force of certainty that wowed out from the crowd, like a voice saying, *here*, in the way that *here* could signal an offering and a place at the same time. Recognition presented itself as a narrowing entrance, like a funnel, leading toward her face while something about her face poured forward. Suddenly the afternoon at the bakery lit up between us. It was Claudia.

¿Qué tal? I said. What's going on?

Her eyes came down from where they wandered unblinking along the branches of the trees.

It's me, the Canadian, I said. I talked with you and Carlos about how you met. Do you remember?

Her head tilted back and throttled down in a giant nod as if she were breaking a piece of wood with her chin. She was in a hurry. She put her hand on my shoulder and opened the door to the print shop.

Inside, she pressed her face against the computer screen as she clicked the mouse in fast patterns that sounded like a Geiger counter, getting closer to something. I printed a story I had written for the next workshop and paid at the desk. Across the room, Claudia shouted and moaned. The owner of the shop shook his head and muttered under his breath. Claudia repeated what she said. The owner shrugged.

She wants to open a page, I said. She's trying to look up the bus schedule to Rosario.

For some reason I understood her easily. I could hear the words beyond the sounds. After I helped her find what she was looking for she still seemed distressed.

I know her, I explained to the man at the desk, who was watching us from across the room.

I can't understand a single word she says, said the owner.

~

People are using fewer and fewer words, said Mariana. But what happens if language keeps shrinking? The experiences that one has of the world can also shrink.

I always think that I'm accumulating words, collecting them, I said. Especially in Spanish, where my living archive of words grows every day. But to have the contrary would be … I trailed off, lacking the language to imagine it.

It's sad, said Mariana. At times I think it's something even harmful. It gives me the sensation that language tends to unify. That people tend to reduce variety. Certain words are used in the media, on both sides, in which the word starts to vacillate in significance. For example, those of Canal 7 are talking about the monopolies of media. They themselves are talking about the media as if they weren't media. So the word itself is filled with other concepts, or it empties of concepts.

discourse is a funnel

meaning is an equilibrium

concepts are substances

Maybe this epoch requires a distinct language, she said. Language expresses a world to you and this world is changing very fast. You look at the heavens and in place of stars you see satellites.

That makes me think again of names, I said. Years ago the name Adrián meant one thing, who I was then, but now it has another sentiment. It contains another. But that word, Adrián, follows me for all my life, even though it goes on changing.

One must flee from the word! Mariana erupted. From the name! Yes, that's terrible. We are prisoners in words.

If only we could elect a different name each morning, I mused.

Is that why we are raised with the concept of "one"? Mariana asked. If you are a multiple being and you are distinct each time, how is it that you have one unique word that names you? It's not only that it names you but it conditions you. For example, if I become Adrián, how am I going to do this?! Adrián would do something else. That name deprives you of your liberty to act. The word can come to limit you.[6]

a name is a condition

creativity is un-naming

~

And yet for me, a mundane word was a wild new freedom. Maybe learning Spanish without studying it in a classroom, without verb tables or grammar lessons, just learning it from the sounds as I heard them used in Chile, Cuba, Nicaragua, Argentina, and countries in between –maybe that was a way of being creative, too, with an art that had been made a billion times in the minds of others already but that was, for the one who learned it, a new act, an absolute birth, a beginning as though there had never been that precise beginning before. All the words existed, all the shapes I wanted were there to be learned from others. To the world I invented nothing, my best work was to sound like anyone else, but to me invention was in every sentence. I woke up in language. I came alive. Creativity cycled privately through every life across time. Maybe creativity was a rhythm.

Long ago, one of the writers I met in Cuba had told me: everybody has eaten an apple, but nobody knows what an apple tastes like to you.

~

Soy Adrián, I said into the gold-coloured buzzer on Chile Street in San Telmo. A woman brought me upstairs, where I unrolled my mat and waited for two others to arrive. The teacher would begin the recitation and I could join whenever I felt ready. She showed me how to sit and gave me a piece of paper with Sanskrit words written on it. Some of the words had a dozen letters; some had even more. When everyone was assembled, we closed our eyes. The teacher started chanting.

At first I had no idea what to say, what noises I could possibly make to participate. Two cycles of the chant went by. When I understood how the first line began and could hear it approaching like a bus coming around the corner, I launched into it but I was so surprised by my own voice that I broke away from the sound as it passed. I joined in when it came back to the start, this time bending into the first vowels and faking it through the middle to clip a solid consonant near the end of the line. Again the chant went around. My voice flexed inward at the start of the words to meet them and fall away in the wide space of their middles where I couldn't make anything out. Some words were not the words themselves but the space between them, so that the word was made more by how the sounds got there than what they did once they arrived. There was one sagging junction in a long trough of vowels that passed again and again without me, so that I dreaded it each time it got closer, knowing I would fail.

The other voices in the room didn't breathe in unison. Instead, they held at their own place, scattering a pattern of pauses over the chant, each person adding their unique silence to one big voice made between us. My own breathing was erratic, ambushing me with sudden need. I pulled off to the side of the chant while it went on without me, circling to catch up when it passed again a minute later. The chase went on for half an hour. I resented the sound of my voice, the grainy, nasal drone that shuddered out of my skull, until one quick moment when everything aligned and I found myself on the inside of sound. I travelled through the space of the chant with the other voices as if we were all one. We were no longer reciting phrases – the phrases were reciting us. They made themselves around us, through us, by, with, and because of us, but beyond us, too. Sound spoke itself freely. The words already existed; we brought them to life. The rhythm did its work. All I had to do was be present.

The teacher rang a tiny gong. Our voices passed into the distance as though we were still reciting the chant in the next room, loops of sound falling over the city. When I finally spoke, my voice was strange.

Gracias, I said to the teacher, dismayed by my lack of momentum and strength. The loops of sound were out of reach.

~

Creativity Is a State of Mind

Juan Diego Incardona[7] spent thirteen years as a street vendor selling earrings and bracelets on the sidewalk at night. Gloria's friend Mercedes had introduced us. They had met at a book launch. His presence was calming, as if he were always waking up from a nap, and he seemed at home wherever he sat down. During those years as a street vendor he wrote in the afternoons while listening to music. Now his schedule had changed but the music was still there.

Music is the mother, he said when we met in the garden of Espacio Cultural Nuestros Hijos, where he worked. All the other arts are the sons and daughters of music. It's first and most in something like creativity. Because I believe that in the moment of writing one is creating a rhythm. A rhythm of sound but also of feeling.

Then he said something that sounded like a riddle: writing is like a semantic rhythm of thrown relations.

Over the course of four books, Juan Diego Incardona had constructed the world of Villa Celina, a suburban neighbourhood on the sprawling outskirts of Buenos Aires. He grew up there. His work as a writer had been to build that life into fiction, often fantastical, by, to use his word, "literaturizing" experiences, anecdotes, characters, and feelings. The scale of the neighbourhood fascinated him, he said, because you are telling part of the history of a country.

What pleases me is to tell the grand political themes, national ones, in the history of the small village, he said.

He added the words of Leo Tolstoy: Paint your village and you paint the world.

Juan Diego's speech was bursting with metaphor. He turned to it easily and developed each image or comparison with comfort and familiarity, as though it were obvious that literary style could be sampled for red-blood cells and that creativity required a collector's eye for rare figurines. After we had settled at a table in the garden at the back of the building complex, I asked him about the role of memory, since it seemed important to the world of Villa Celina.

How good, he said with earnest enthusiasm. Yes, evidently creativity is like the reunion of various vital forces. And one of the prevailing ones in my case is experience. I didn't always write like this. At one time I injected myself with the serum of the library, and I tried to imitate the literature of those that I admired. For example, as a boy I read a lot of Borges and inevitably I copied Borges.

As I advanced, he continued, I contaminated my memories with imagination. I even exacerbated them, bound them up in the fantastic.

Contaminate in what sense? I asked, still enjoying the image of a library in a syringe.

Contaminate not pejoratively, he clarified, but in the sense that they are not facts, that it's literature.

What I was doing didn't have many antecedents in Argentine literature, he explained. There isn't much written about the suburbs of Buenos Aires. In the last few years there have appeared a few writers who are working on it, but not many. The proper name, Villa Celina, plays a very strong role in my work. It's a place that exists. The names of the streets appear, names of people that exist. The operation was to literaturize a segmented zone of reality that has a cartography that exceeds the geographic and includes a culture, that is, the popular culture.

~

I wasn't trying to compare myself to Juan Diego, but memory played a vital role in what I was trying to do, too. There were many points from which to write about an experience and each of them was true, but the truth of the experience could not be sought in its writing. For whether I wrote about an experience in the moment I had it, jotting a note in the little book I always kept in my pocket, or months later when I revisited those notes with prose, I depended on memory. That night when I was searching for Isabel, trying to find her for the first time, and on my way to the venue I had seen the shadow of a leafless tree cast upon a grey brick wall, it crossed my mind that the shadow was a crack in the stone, a thick break that started at the sidewalk and splintered as it reached the sky. *Shadow = crack in wall*, I wrote, and tucked my notebook back in my pocket.

Memory was exercised twice in that account. The first time was nearly simultaneous with the experience. I saw the shadow of the tree, perceived something of language that could be used to tag the experience, and wrote it down. In that case the muscle of memory performed more of a spasm than a flex. I wrote quickly and kept moving. Weeks later I would be back in Canada, sitting at a desk in Vancouver, remembering the shadow of the tree against the wall as if peering through a little window made by the notes.

Memory was performing in a longer way, longer because I spent more time writing it than I did on the
day I saw it, and longer in the sense that I stretched
back through time to reach the point when the experience was first drawn. Neither one of those accounts
was more or less true than the other, but they were
different, a difference that was felt as much by the
tone of their telling as by the quantity of their content. Reading one or the other, the note or the prose,
gave a different texture to an experience that was
somehow beyond the reach of either of them. The
words became things of their own, tethered to an invisible past. Each metaphor for creativity did the
same: a variation on an original, always out of reach.

~

It is important to me that the work brings something
new, said Juan Diego. That literature isn't simply a
copy of other anterior literature. Because it's one
thing to inscribe yourself in a tradition, in literary systems of interpretation, for example the literature of
the periphery, or of Peronism, or literature that works
with rock music, politics, or love. But an author must
put forward with the language, with the themes, with
the treatment of those themes, something that's his
or her own. That's where there's different value from
the rest. If not, we would simply be copying one another and accumulating common places in literature,
because the common places are comfortable. What's
good is to assume the risk of bringing raw material. creativity is an outlier
Material that has little literature.

It's like the little figurines, he explained. I don't
know if in Canada you collect figurines when you are
kids. Kids here have little figures of the players from

soccer teams. Boca Juniors for example. River, Boca, those are the most well-known teams in Argentina. The number ten of Boca or the number ten of River are in many collections because they are famous. But the difficult figurines are the number four of Temperley, the number four of Bánfield, the little clubs. It's the unique place where the little players are worth more than those that in reality are worth millions. And the other figurine is a guy who maybe makes just enough to live, but that one is worth more. You find very few of those. In literature it's the same. I'm not going to look for the number ten of Boca, I'm going to look for the number four of Bánfield or the number four of Sacachispas, which is a really small club in the neighbourhood. That is to say, I'm going to find the diamond in the carbon.

creativity is collecting

creativity is pressure

I was surprised by how easily Juan Diego used metaphor to describe his ideas. In my introduction to the project, when we first sat down for the conversation, I told him that I was interested in narrative accounts of his creative process. I didn't mention anything about metaphor, not wanting to lead the conversation toward it too explicitly. But it seemed that he already knew what I was looking for and offered it to me constantly. It was as though he thought in metaphor.

The search is permanent, he added. It never ends.

creativity is solitude

The less literature there is behind what you're doing, the more potent the creativity will be, he continued. Because if there are already heavy books from grand authors, the chances for creativity are crushed. Those grand voices asphyxiate you.

a voice is a force that liberates

Now, he said, when someone puts themselves in a terrain that is a desert terrain, where one is walking for the first time, it's not that Borges, Cortázar, Bioy

Cesares, Kafka, Beckett were walking around there, no. It's a place where I construct the road and where creativity has the possibility of good results.

creativity is a road in the desert

~

As in writing, as in metaphor, communicating an experience transformed it into words. But that didn't mean it couldn't become something new again and again.

On a different day I wrote in my notebook: (1) man = charcoal. Before that there was an experience, true only to itself. The words were a tag, a way of marking the moment so that I could find it again in the archive of my memory. Apparently, what happened before and after was less interesting, or didn't convert so easily into language. Some moments declared themselves.

When I got home that day I flipped through my notebook and from that equation I wrote the following (2): Walked along Rivadavia with my printed stories in a folder under my arm. Stopped to eat an *empanada* leaning against a building. A man like a smudge of charcoal, carrying a tremendous garbage bag over his shoulder, mumbled at me, asking why I wouldn't give him something to eat. I gave him the other half of my food.

Now the process was in motion, the one where an experience of life unfolded into words, which unfolded into more words, expanding outward beyond their start, growing, and with each incarnation changing. Like the next version, which I wrote months later, unfolding the moment again: (3) It was dusk and I was late for the writing workshop, hurrying along Rivadavia and looking ahead to each corner for a bakery where I could eat something without slowing down. I was riding on my legs as if they were a steady animal, the rest of me slumped above my hips.

One *empanada*, I said, facing the smell of bread, and the words were also a thought as I considered how much I could eat, how the food would fit in the room of my body.

I hadn't seen anyone in Buenos Aires walk and eat at the same time – it just wasn't done, even if here and there a final bite were swallowed in the space between a café and a *colectivo*. No, in this city you stood still if you had to eat on the sidewalk. Even children outside school or playing in a park, I confirmed, stopped moving to eat.

Complying with the silent law, I leaned against the wall in the entrance to an alley, not wanting to draw attention, wanting to belong, but eating as fast as I could, knowing that each bite made me later for class. A man shuffled along the sidewalk carrying a bulging garbage bag over his shoulder, his clothes looking like burnt wood. I knew that he could see things that nobody else could see; I knew he would see me. I chewed so hard my temples hurt.

Why won't you give me something to eat? the man said.

My throat went dry and my eyes watered. Suddenly I couldn't swallow. Years ago, the same thing had happened to me in Chile: a man with clothes like an old fire asked my friend for food and without hesitating my friend broke what he was eating in half and shared it. The gesture was so confident, so basic, that it was a long clear note from an instrument I had never heard but instantly understood. I even wondered if this was the same man, if all the charcoal men of the world would appear in patterns, wanting food or money, just as I would appear again and again as a stranger in the street, and this encounter would play itself out across time until I learned what to do with it.

The thought of my friend gave me courage, like a breeze. He was showing me a way out, a way beyond. The man hadn't moved.

Why won't you give me something to eat?

I shared my food.

And so another image of that first written moment folded out. From two words and a sign, *man = charcoal*, two words that were also signs, as Derrida would have said, a wider glimpse opened. That glimpse was widened again to another image. Neither one was truer than the others – they were each iterations of a moment that would never be repeated, never really be conveyed, only altered by the tools of language. I could say even that language deformed the experience. Maybe the only truth was that *something happened*.

Each account, whether three words or three hundred, had an invisible partner in the past – the lived moment that would never be seen again except in the language that was attached to it. The two separate entities of experience and language were tethered together in the act of metaphor making: experience was the topic and language was the vehicle. Metaphor was that generative gap between the world as it was and the world as it could be. More metaphors equalled more worlds.

~

The grey city swept by with pools of yellow light between the trees, the kind of light that made me want to lean my head against the taxi window and look up, tired but alive, as I had seen someone do in a movie while the reflections of buildings and the pale blue glow of dawn glided in liquid bubbles across the glass. I was passing through Boedo. It might have been four o'clock in the morning.

Here, said the driver, wrenching on the brake, Bar de Roberto.

Almost asleep, I stood on the sidewalk while the taxi drifted away. Part of me was still curled up in the back seat as it left, the part of me that was homeward, so that when the taxi was really gone I was left with what remained: the part that had no home and wasn't going anywhere, that never slept even though it was exhausted, because it had no place to sleep, moving with its eyes closed, feeling with the hands of a soul that had no body. The city spread out from that one place on the concrete.

Shadows spilled from a black rectangular hole in the wall. Wanting to keep moving, wanting to have a reason to move, I turned to the two people I had come with, Gloria and Mercedes, the ones I had had dinner with and stayed up late talking and drinking wine with, intending to ask them, ¿todo bien? All good? and nod in solidarity, but I couldn't see them. I looked around. A tree loomed at the corner of the sidewalk. Yellow light fell through the branches to break in patterns on the ground. The red dot of a cigarette lit up against the trunk and for a second the little light breathed in on a face, then was gone.

Had they left in the taxi? Had they left without me?

My head spun. I went through the gestures and sounds we had made while getting out: the rustle for money in the dim taxi light, my foot on the pavement to stand at the curb. Three doors slammed. I was sure they were here.

I walked toward the shadowy hole of the entrance to the bar, wearing a sense of purpose like a jacket that had belonged to an older brother. Someone lifted their arm with the cigarette hanging above my head. I passed underneath.

Inside the bar it was so dark I could barely see. I didn't want to stand still to look around. It would make it obvious that I didn't know where I was going, and if I didn't know that then maybe I didn't belong. I felt the balance in my body, the balls of my feet and the pads of my toes, the shifting weight in my bones. There were narrow spaces made by the absence of chairs and tables, chunks of openness that I drifted into like a current of air in a still room, hovering, waiting, but waiting with intention. When a space opened I moved into it and found myself on the other side of the room. But what room?

A door even blacker than the first went away into nothing. I could hear small rough voices echoing off the walls as though they were reflections of candlelight on the cement, all texture, no source. Finally looking into the space I had crossed, back the way I had come, I saw the shadow of a man tending a long bar with bottles stacked up high behind him, so high he could never have reached the upper ones. I saw why it was so dark: there was no more than a single light bulb high above at the top of the room. The light that it cast was thin and tired by the time it reached the floor. It seemed only strong enough to trace a little grey line across the tops of the hunched blobs of darkness below. Then a man started singing.

He didn't so much sing as tear his soul open. Inside him there was an animal made of ink and pain. But inside that, because it seemed he was shedding layer after layer so that every time he made a sound another animal roared and whimpered beyond that one – inside all of those, at the very centre, was the man again, so infinite he stood alone with rules broken around him, as if they were the egg shells from which he had been born. He was wearing a suit. His white shirt was dishevelled, stained with night, and his jacket was unkempt like ripped wings after a century of forgetting how to fly. His face, a sagging puddle of grey, looked up as though the rest of him wanted to see out from under his eyelids, eyelids that refused to open all the way because his body had fallen asleep a long time ago and his voice, this voice that was climbing out of him through a hole in his heart, wanted up toward the light. He stood on a chair and wobbled, swooning, holding a glass cup to his chest. He stuck out his chin and gestured with his cup at all the suffering in the room.

It was then that I noticed a man playing guitar beside his table. I hadn't heard him before, only felt that he was there, that something else was in the room with the voice. I leaned against the wall and listened. A young man with a forest of black curly hair tilted a wine bottle at me, raising his eyebrows. Beside the bottle there was a glass that looked as if it had been traced into the room with white chalk. He poured me a cup of wine and nodded, lifting his own glass, not to me but to the man who was singing, and we both drank while the song cut holes in the night.

The singer's eyes were closed now. He clawed at his shirt. Stars of spit fell in the air. He faced the floor, his mind gone and his body left over to die. Then he rose and stamped his foot on the table. His head threw open to drink, ready to swallow the whole glass, hurling it into the fire of his mouth to smash at the back of his throat where the flames were. The song was an ending, even from the very first word. When it was over he fell asleep with his head against the guitar player's chest.

My feeble project returned: to call what he had done "creative" was insulting. His life had burned up in a song.

I left the bar, expelled into night. The sidewalk felt even emptier than before. Home was a faraway sound or a candle on a hill. I moved toward it. The street yawned, a deep black maw. I went back to stand by the doorway of the bar, leaning against the wall, watching nothing, waiting for nothing. The city vanished and there was only this one corner in the night. Voices tinkled from the darkness. I thought of the other door at the back of the room, the one I hadn't entered. In the taxi I leaned my head against the window, looking up at the dawn.

~

Juan Diego was not the only author to create a literary universe and set his stories within it. We talked about William Faulkner's Yoknapatawpha Country, Gabriel García Márquez's Macondo, Juan Rulfo's haunted plains of northern Mexico.

Is Villa Celina a world that you have already fixed, I asked, or does it go along changing by way of the writing?

Yes, by way of the writing it transforms but I'm conscious when I work, said Juan Diego. It's not instinctive. What's instinctive is perhaps the imagination, but there's a program. There's a plan in all this work, this

history is a conversation   universe, where I dialogue with the tradition of Argentine literature. In my books, for example, the characters of Leopoldo Marechal, Roberto Arlt, Borges, and Héctor Oersterheld appear. It pleases me to inscribe myself in a tradition. It's good from the perspective of the ludic, too, that creativity plays with tradition and inscribes a belonging.

creativity is play

writing is membership

Because to write is also to belong, he added. To belong to something. To a social community, a literary community, a camaraderie.

Like a carpenter with wood, the author thinks that there are things that serve him more than others, said Juan Diego. He discards some wood and takes others because they are good for the universe. Not everything enters the universe, or there are some things that prosper more than others.

I asked him how he knew what wood to keep and what wood to throw away. Was that an instinct? He gave me another metaphor instead.

Creativity is a stream of water. The writer's technique – how they produce characters, the scenes, how they produce verisimilitude, with what tone they work the realism or the lack of realism, the atmosphere, the climate, the suspense – all that is what shapes the stream of water. How to make the pipe smaller, for example, so that it comes out with more pressure and doesn't become a lagoon. It's like a sentimental disorder, he said. But one can direct it a little, no?

creativity is a liquid

Soon enough there are leaks, he added. The pipe bursts, and that's what is beautiful about literature, that it's an experience.

~

I had brunch at Silvia's house in San Telmo with the sunlight coming blunt and wide through the fourth-floor windows, surrounded by her collection of paintings and musical instruments.

I was exhausted, my body a deflated bag of air slumped at the table as I clung to the only idea I could think of: stay upright. My eyes were sour little knots and my stomach was fluttery and open as if it had been lifted into a place in my chest. The pride I had felt in getting home at five o'clock in the morning the night before had turned to numbness, too tired even to judge the person I had been when I made the decision to stop at Bar de Roberto to hear a man wrench out his whisky-soaked heart in the form of a tango. Now, in morning light, it was as though that city, that person, that feeling, was a dream.

There, said Silvia when we had finished eating. Now read me what you've written.

I had promised I would share my latest story. I moved into the voice of the language as if I lived there, taking up the sounds with a confidence that seemed to come from the words themselves; and not just from the words, which on their own were, in a way, meaningless, but from the intonation that held them together. It was the sounds between the words, the way one word moved into the next, that gave me strength.

I channelled all the times I had heard men read out loud in Buenos Aires, filtering those moments for the ones that were humble, dignified, and clear, as though I were looking up at a mountaintop that I hoped one day to climb. To read I had to suspend the part of my mind that understood meaning and give in, blindly, but seeing in a way that was blind, to a constant relay from the words to the sounds. I saw and spoke, transforming sight into sound.

Then I faltered. My tongue caught. I ran over the word again and again until Silvia said it for me. I repeated it badly, crestfallen, betrayed by the language I had chosen. Yet there was triumph when I finished, wanting more.

Very good, Silvia said like a teacher. The ending especially has something. The beginning takes too long but that's me.

She removed an anthology from the shelf and showed me her name beneath one of the poems, standing up to read it with her chair tucked in beside the table. I was relieved that one image stood out and I could cleave to it until the poem was finished so I could repeat it back to her. Otherwise the work was lost on me. I had never known what a poem was, partly because I didn't know what a poem wasn't. Later I decided that it was a poem if it ached with what was not there, but in this case I couldn't understand enough of what was there to know what was missing and consequently nothing ached. The sounds, however, ached just a little on their own.

To the park, then? said Silvia, putting on her scarf.

The sunlight at Puerto Madero was cool and dry, already laying itself out flat next to the long shadows of trees. After we had walked for an hour, so slowly that we meandered in little circles to keep from falling over, Silvia stopped and lifted her face to the sun. She closed her eyes. I stood beside her with my hands in my pockets. When she showed no sign of moving, I copied her. With my eyes closed I could see the two of us as if from the perspective of people walking past, people whose lives I knew only from the sound of their footsteps and the things they said as they walked. What little I heard was calibrated by the tone of their voice and the patter of a dog's paws on the paving stones before they were gone, so that I could invent an entire attitude just from the way someone said, *che ¿entendés?*, an attitude that was more like a feeling or an orientation, a position, that dissolved into air when the sound of another life moved past. Light soaked red and black into my eyelids. My neck was bare and brave. Only the thoughts of others held me in the world, held me down like a net. Across my cheeks spread not heat but a glow that started at my skin and went into my muscles. My face went slack, like a hand that finally lets go of a heavy bag that until then has been cutting into the fingers and still burns, but burns because it is coming back to life.

When I opened my eyes, Silvia had wandered away in the direction of home, her steps scribbling lazy loops on the white stones.

I'm going back now, she called, my ankle hurts. But you should stay. I can see that you need this.

I walked for two more hours with the Rio Plata stretching to the east – an hour away until my feet hurt, so tired that I stubbed my toes on the paving stones, and an hour home, which, because of my fatigue and because the sun had gone down between the buildings, left the same trace as a thought or a friend or a poem.

~

Do you believe you have achieved your style? I asked. Do you already know what it is?

No, Juan Diego paused. I have a universe. Style is something that's in permanent transformation. Because it goes along varying. The grammar is getting richer, it's incorporating other things. It's subtle at times but what's mine is the universe. An author's style is in permanent growth. If you don't achieve this transformation you repeat yourself. It's like one becomes redundant, monotonous. It's difficult for authors who find a recipe, a formula, and they stay there, trapped. They don't try to put in new things.

I thought of something Guillermo Martínez had said: in learning to write one book you learn to write many others like it. Each book must set off alone.

You know those authors whose names convert into adjectives? said Juan Diego. Borges, borgesian. Kafka, kafkesque. It is because they have achieved something that is of them. It's like if you took a blood sample from them, let's say, from a ten-page short story you take a sample from page two. It's going to have the same quantity of red blood cells, of vitamins, that speaks of

language is wealth

convention is a container

style is blood, creativity is life force

the whole body. The same if you had taken it from page four or five. It doesn't matter what moment of the story it's from. There's something of the style of the author that's their own and that has the quantity of red blood cells, white blood cells.

I went along aspiring to find mine, Juan Diego explained, my own mode of expressing myself, which is difficult because one has to break with all the idioms that are not one's own. And this original idiom, it's not totally new. Instead it's a new combination of all the others. It's how much you put of this idiom, how much of this one, how much of that one. What reading each person has had; the writer and the reader. What things one elects from life. How does he or she observe the world. It depends.

language is a connection

creativity is an algorithm

~

The next day I went to the massive park near Plaza Italia in Palermo and walked long slow laps around the lake while radiantly beautiful people clattered past on rollerblades. Families spread out on the grass. I sat under a tree and tried to read. Nothing came. The world of the writing was not enough and instead I looked emptily at the world going by, feeling distant from both of them, the book and the world. Surely there was someone I could call.

I thought of Pilar from the writing workshop and how she had secretly sent me one of her stories. It was the account of a nun who started to notice one of the boys who lit the candles in the church and she didn't know what to do with her feelings. I was grateful and wished that we could already know each other in a way that was honest. Then, when I saw her again at the workshop, she did not look at me. I imagined her standing over me, tearing my stories into strips that fell through the cold sunlight as she smiled.

In the middle of the park was a gallery showing the drawings of the Hungarian artist Lajos Szalay. His grotesque figures climbed from the shadows where the roof met the trees, a giant white foot looming over the park while shattered lines erupted through one of the windows. I wanted to take his drawings with me, not as much for how they looked as for how it felt to see them. Standing there in the gallery, I suddenly believed I could do it: I had something to say with art. The purpose of drawing wasn't to supplant the things I had seen. The drawings would exist on their own terms. Part of the world, apart from the world.

The sun went down and the park closed, not only as a place but as an idea and I could no longer remember it, reaching back through my notes in another time. I made my way into the city, not wanting to go home. I walked up Jorge Luis Borges Street to Plazoleta Cortázar and wandered around Palermo Viejo in the twilight. Everyone had someone to visit. Leaning against the window of a shop that sold handbags, I watched people walk by. For a long time I didn't see anything. I was imagining the drawings I would make. Even in my imagination, none of them came out right. Without notice or reason, I pushed off and walked back toward the subway station.

~

Do you believe that creativity can be learned? I asked.

It can be stimulated, said Juan Diego. I believe there are things that are innate, that have to do with some people's capacity for observation. Others have much imagination. Others have a good sense of rhythm. But it can be stimulated. Practice or a good workshop can stimulate it. Maybe the simplest things to learn in a workshop are techniques, because they are more tangible, more concrete. I can explain what a determined narrative process signifies so that you practise it, but I'm not able to teach that person a mode of imagination. To me it seems that it has a lot to do with how one was moulded in their infancy, the imagination of infancy. Because to write literature is to be a little bit a child, to play with things.

When I asked him what he did in the moments when he didn't know how to continue what he was writing, he told me about learning to play the guitar.

The first time you touch the guitar you are doing scales the whole time, he said. Do, re, mi, fa, sol. You bore yourself doing scales. Until a moment when the hand flies on the fretboard and you are no longer looking at your fingers so that they press well. You forget about the left hand and you lend your attention to the right hand, which is the hand of interpretation. The left now goes on its own. It has the technique. And here you interpret the song, with the right. But first you have to do a lot of practice.

music is contact

Our conversation closed with humility.

It's a vocation, said Juan Diego. It calms me to have written this about my neighbourhood where I lived for thirty years, which has to do with my family, my friends, my culture. If I'm going to die today, among all the messes that I made, if there's something I did clean it was to write these books. I'm tranquil for having done something in which I put everything: love, values … I feel that vocationally I achieved a result that satisfies me. And many times that doesn't happen. Many times I studied things that I abandoned. But here I constructed a universe and it's the fruit of much work. Many hours of solitude. You have to be there at home, writing, when everyone else is having a party.

creativity is food

But it was worth the shame because today people read these things. A kid reads them. Or you come from another country and you read them. It's magical.[8]

~

Later, when all that remained of Buenos Aires were feelings and even those had softened to the point where I had to turn them into words to preserve some semblance of what they had been, I made charcoal drawings of my host Eugenio from the photos I had taken while he and I had dinner. I wished there was a reason why I didn't use ink as in the drawings I had seen in the park near Plaza Italia, a principled, aesthetic reason, and if I tried to invent one I would have said it was because ink seemed to show itself in terms that were too certain, too clear, and what I felt required a kind of mental massaging to understand it. I was still thinking of the charcoal drawings I had seen with Silvia in La Boca. Maybe that was why. But the reason was probably simpler than that. I already knew what to do with charcoal. I understood how it behaved. Plus, I could get my hands dirty and massage the drawing in the same way I hoped to do figuratively with my memories.

The drawings helped me understand what I had been searching for all along in language. By drawing Eugenio, I carried the image of his face from something literal, from the photograph, to something intuitive, something less concrete, in the drawing. The drawings didn't look exactly like him. I had the photographs for that. Instead, I used them for ideas about how light fell across a face and the kinds of shadows it made. I wanted to give in to the way his image could be interpreted by the medium. Charcoal exerted its own force over the outcome. If I had used ink, it would have become something else, because ink had its own authority, too. Each drawing incarnated the photograph in a unique way. I was carrying the photograph beyond itself into an image that was connected to its literal appearance by certain traits, while taking on new ones because of the medium, because of decisions I made, because of my hopes and inadequacies and intuitions.

To put it in terms of language, the photograph was the topic and the drawing was the vehicle of the visual utterance. They were bound by similarities of meaning – maybe the drawn eyes had something in common with the photographed eyes – and held apart by differences. In no two drawings did Eugenio look like the same person, as though each interpretation became something else.

Metaphor was like that too. I coupled the word "creativity" with different experiences to see what new understandings the metaphor could create. Creativity was the literal object, the topic in the phrase, the equivalent of the photograph. Contact, chance, confession, and other variations were the recast object, the vehicle, the drawing.

No drawing was ever the last drawing, just as no metaphor was the last metaphor. There could always be others, and each one would make something else of the photograph as long as no two drawings were identical. Luckily, there were many factors that prevented any two drawings from ever being the same: the medium, the timing, the focus, the hope, my own inconsistency, and more; the possibility of talent, the journey of the artist, the incubation of the idea, the epiphany of the image, the strategy of the layering, the possession of the mind, the madness of the line, the vulnerability of the intention, the mortality I wished to eschew, the tension and attunement that kept me trying. In short, expanding the metaphorical range, just like making drawings from photographs, was a creative act.

But that process didn't start with the photograph. In its own way, the photograph was already a transposition of the original. The photograph, after all, was taken from life. Eugenio and I ate dinner together in a world that really happened and, from it, I took a picture. That picture isolated some aspects of Eugenio's lived person and let go of others. It did not convey, for example, the way he swung his head when he looked up at the television from peeling an orange. There was no trace of the smell of cigarettes or how he waved the knife he used to chop cabbage while acting out the Spanish accent of the losing soccer team. The noise he made – Hup! – when he was startled in the kitchen was silenced. Time was replaced by impossible stillness.

The photograph of Eugenio was not Eugenio. It was connected to him by the similarities between the physical aspect of his lived appearance and his photographed one. There was an experience and an image, connected by the mind that brought one to the other, a mind that made metaphor by carrying the unsaid experience beyond itself into language. It was the same with this very text, this written account of my time in Buenos Aires: it was *of* me, but it was not me. A variation. A possibility. An invitation to be otherwise. In Borges's story, "Las Ruinas Circulares" (The Circular Ruins), the narrator set out to bring something original into the world: "The purpose which guided him was not impossible, though supernatural. He wanted to dream a man; he wanted to dream him in minute entirety and impose him on reality."[9] I was that man, dreamer and dreamed. Even the author was fiction.

After all, how could I really share the experience when it was so complex, full of sound and smell and time? Something was always left out of the record. Looking back through the pinhole of retrospect, I believe that the photograph allowed me to consider Eugenio anew. Drawing him was a way to look closely. Each iteration of transformation – from life to photograph to drawing to other drawings, to other languages – offered an opportunity for the wisdom of metaphor, using something that was not the thing to consider the thing, using B to consider the possibilities of A. The process of making metaphors showed what B and A were capable of together. Maybe it was no coincidence that those were the initials of the city where I had chosen to ask what it meant to be creative.

I had a final thought about the drawings, and here I would let metaphor do the talking. One thing I learned along the way, one thing that blew my mind and completely changed the way I worked with charcoal, showing me how highlights could be bright where I wanted them and how contrast drew the eye through the image; one thing that changed my practice, lending control and the confidence to abandon what I had thought were rules, was a rubbery little nugget that I could mould into any shape I needed, wiping away what hadn't worked and making a neat line out of a smudge. Just as a story was made by leaving things out, so was every charcoal drawing lit with absence. I recommend for any aspiring artist a really good eraser.

~

Creativity Is a Dance

I met Vanesa Guerra at a bar in Palermo after dinner. Mariana Docampo had connected us, after our conversation a few weeks before. By now, I knew how to introduce my project. I used fewer words but ones that mattered more and my sentences had decisive endings. I lit up when the interviews began, assuming the role of host, and took on confidence I had until then only imagined was mine.

Vanesa was a psychoanalyst and an author of short stories, although, like Mariana, she didn't care for the term "stories." Soon enough she would tell me why. I was touched that she brought a notebook and a pen to our conversation, as though she hoped to collect new ideas, too. I began by asking about a line that had stood out in her book, *La Sombra del Animal* (The Shadow of the Animal).

In the short piece called "Las Alas" (The Wings), you wrote: "Nuestra poca fuerza reside en eso, en un falso no saber, en un falso no querer saber. En la práctica de un olvido inmediato"[10] (Our little force resides in that, in a false not-knowing, in a false not-

wanting-to-know. In the practice of an immediate forgetting). It made me wonder if at times this is also the
process of writing. That writing demands a certain
forgetting to be able to continue writing. Without that
forgetting, self-consciousness impedes us.

Enchanting, said Vanessa. It had never occurred to
me to put it that way. Your reading pleases me.

She reread her own phrases out loud.

It's true, she smiled.

From there our talk seemed to travel in all directions at once, and only later did I realize that there
was a central force that held those directions in place.
Understanding Vanesa's words was like the difference
between looking at the fragmented light that casts off
from the faces of a prism, and looking at the prism itself. Our conversation spun the prism. At first all I
could see were frantic blasts of dazzling light. When I
calmed I could see the steady shape at its centre.

It's as if writing were a mode of untangling something that's in a very intuitive order, said Vanesa, that
exists as if it were a dream. You see that one dreams
and when one tells that dream, you have already done
a torsion. You put it into words.

writing is translating
non-language
into language

You add things, she said. It's as if by writing it you
are changing the material.

non-language is a
material, the material
changes with words

To me it seems that the creative act is how we translate ourselves, she continued. It takes us from one
place and puts us in another, where one doesn't stay
the same. At least it happens to me that I don't stay
the same, in myself. It produces a species of exile.

translation is exile

Not by way of stories, she added. To me the stories
don't matter. In truth, they are not important to me. I
am not a grand raconteur of stories. I prefer that they
are told to me by others. What I do is different. I believe that writing is like returning to a zone where we
are not inhabited by language.

~

My tango lessons were in the basement of a café on Avenida San Juan. The café was open in the evenings when I arrived but closed when I left, so that after the lessons I climbed out into the street through a tiny door beside the main entrance.

I usually arrived before Patricia, my teacher. I waited with the quiet relief of someone who had a reason to be there even though I looked the same as the ones who had no reason at all. When she arrived, Patricia's smile seemed covered by a curtain of fatigue which, at times, blew away to reveal her true face, radiant and kind, before the curtain fell back again. She lived alone and had a twenty-year-old daughter on the other side of the city.

Patricia wore a big backpack slung over her shoulder that made her lean to one side when she walked. She greeted the owner of the café, a thick bald man with a striped apron, and nodded at me.

¿Bajamos? she said when it was time to go down the stairs.

Show me what you know, she said at our first lesson. She had taken off her scarf and her jacket and set up little speakers from her computer.

I held my hand behind her back, hovering at her spine.

Stay light, she said. Don't lead with your hand, lead with your torso.

I searched for the place in my body that would turn us from the centre. It felt as though I were rummaging in the dark of my chest, digging with my mind, until we finally turned. We danced around the broken tiles of the basement.

Tango is no more than two people walking together, said Patricia, lifting her hand from my hand and her other hand from where it was resting behind my neck so I was holding her but she was no longer holding me. She turned her head to the side to look at the way we were still moving together.

You see? Just walking.

It was true. We were walking together. Then the weight of my body suddenly became the most complex thing I had ever experienced, a lumbering pendulum swinging side to side with each step. My unweighted hip slipped behind as if my body was advancing without it. When I stepped again my leg pulled in behind. The sound of my shoe slid to catch up along the tiles, barely touching my other shoe as it brushed next to it, advancing into the weighted air of the place where Patricia's body had been.

Knees, was all she said.

Through the next step, I kept my weight slung in my hips and glided the other leg forward, this time making sure that my knees nearly brushed when they passed.

Good, she said. Now, with your hand behind your back.

She withdrew her right hand from my left, and I folded my arm away. We continued. I tried to think from the core of my body.

Deja de pensar, she said.

It would have meant "stop thinking" except that *dejar* was also the verb "to leave," leave thinking, as if thought were a place I could abandon to spend time elsewhere. As if thinking were not the only home I knew, a home I was frightened to leave and had so little practice leaving that when I did, as in the moments of dancing, when the air seemed to break apart and I was stepping through a smile in my mind to an infinite space, something broke in my heart, too, and I wanted to laugh and to cry. The more I tried to leave thinking the more anxious I became so that hearing the words, leave thinking, brought me closer to the edge of dancing but it couldn't push me over. How to let go of wanting to let go?

Once, I drank wine before one of my lessons, hoping it would help me find the abandon I knew was possible from other times dancing, in other cities in other ways. Maybe a drink would make it easier to leave thinking, to soften the edge so that I could tumble, finally, into the ephemeral fluidity that I craved. But it only made it more difficult to find my body.

Where's your weight? said Patricia.

It shifted to different places in my body, at times in my knees and then, just when I thought I had found it, high up across my shoulders so that I could feel it but couldn't settle it anywhere, much less in the centre of my body or, where it belonged, in the music. The pendulum swung wider.

The lesson ended. We climbed through the tiny little door that the owner of the café had left open and walked slowly along the sidewalk to Peru Street, stopping at a barred window where Patricia bought cigarettes and lit one as we continued.

I can tell right away what kind of person someone is by how they dance, she said.

I confessed that I was trapped among thousands of rules that I had made for myself, trying to pre-empt her assessment.

Yes, you dance stiffly. Your shoulders are tight. But here's what I see.

She gave me her backpack to hold.

This is how you danced when you first came to me.

She lurched a few steps with locked knees and her arms up like a robot stopping traffic.

This is how you dance now.

Her body softened. She walked forward, just walking, with her arms embracing a ghost.

You see? she said, squinting into her cigarette and lifting her backpack.

I see a person with a lot of tenderness. It's good that you have it for tango, because that part cannot be taught.

~

To me it seems that we have all had experiences of a non-tongue, a non-language, Vanesa explained. And to me it seems that this non-language is paradoxically the perfect language. It includes the possibility of being multiple at the same time, equivocal, ambiguous. Such an experience stays with you at the limits of language, in permanent orbit. And sometimes through a crack it enters, arrives, connects.

language is a territory that includes the stars

As Vanesa spoke I imagined a stone skipping across the surface of an endless lake at night. The stone was a word. The other side of the lake was impossible to describe.

The original idiom, I said.

Clearly, said Vanesa. The original idiom. It enters as if it were a memory of a language belonging to someone else. When it enters, it enters like an impulse from the heart, an intuition. It arrives like lightning. It seems to me that the creative act has to do with this encounter. The encounter with what goes orbiting around the tongue, around language, because really I believe that it wasn't lost.

creativity is an encounter with non-language

Hearing Vanesa speak was like walking into echoes. I could feel the original sound beyond them even though I hadn't heard it yet.

When it comes close to us, she said, one possibility is to take it and to make it into a translation. I believe this is what art does in all of its manifestations. Another possibility is to not do anything, no? Have a son, plant a tree ... I don't know.

How do you know when that moment has arrived? I asked. How do you know if you are encountering non-language?

I believe that this happens to everyone, said Vanesa, from what I hear from my patients. There are moments in which something that isn't from this world touches them or touches us. It can be testified after in some way. Now if someone is thinking of art, if they are a musician, a writer, a poet, a painter, a sculptor ... that's how to sustain the lightning.

creativity is contact

In this way inspiration is posterior, she said. It's what makes you sustain the material. After inspiration is work, but I don't know if it interests everyone. To in-

spire yourself or to keep inspired, which is more vol-
untary ... it seems to me that it implies work with the
soul, with the spirit.

I never planted it like this before, Vanesa added.
I am planting it for the first time now that I am telling you.

I thought of Walter Benjamin's lightning bolt again,
this time as an encounter with non-language. Inspiration came after it like thunder, sustaining the memory of electric contact. Writing was the long labour of
naming lightning.

ideas are seeds

~

At my lesson the following week, Patricia said I needed
to work on my embrace.

So? she said. Embrace me.

I embraced her.

That is all it is, she said.

As soon as I call it a dance it becomes something
else, I said.

It is just an embrace, she said. Two people walking
together, embracing.

She cleared her backpack off the chair and moved
her computer to the floor. Hold this chair over your
head, like this, she said.

Like this? I asked.

With your hands here.

Okay.

And walk. Just walk.

Like this.

Head up. Like that. Shoulders, shoulders. Relax. When
you embrace me you look like this.

She mimicked me.

That bad?

Strong and relaxed, that's what you want. When you get tired just put it down.

I walked around the basement holding the chair above my head by its legs, my shoulders down and my head up, feeling the weight in my back. When it was over my body leaned back because I was finally standing up straight.

Better, said Patricia.

~

When we name a word, said Vanesa, when we name anything, we put it in a category. Before the word, even before the conformation of "I," time and space are not established. Time and space construct themselves to the extent that they gain terrain for an anterior experience.

time and space are
territories

The way that babies connect to one another is evidence of this non-language, she continued. We could think that there is a language there, without a doubt, but it doesn't have the density of the word. Even if the word is a subtle material, in relation to this non-language it's very dense. So I believe that inspiration, the work of inspiration, is to try to leave behind as much as possible the density of the word.

language is an object

inspiration is the
lightening of words

How can this be done? I asked.

One way is to use words wrongly, she said. To break with certain codes of narrative structures, to shatter certain systems of identity in order to liberate. It seems to me that in those games there is a meaningful effect. That permits you to be a bridge.

So far we have been talking about the word as something unique, I said. What about writing, which

is the union of many words? Do we arrive at something more subtle when we see it in total?

I hope so ... I hope so, said Vanesa. For example, it
seems to me such an arrival happened in me as a
reader of Clarice Lispector, in *The Passion According to
G.H.* In that reading, I had an experience of another
zone outside of language. It seems to me that the
grand works that are involved with that search, they
achieve it. But I don't know if all us writers have that
capacity to achieve it. Clarice achieves it like nobody
else.

So one returns to the origin and brings an impression of that origin back with them, in the form of
words, I said. Is that the journey?

Yes, clearly, said Vanesa. One returns, but one cannot stay there. One must leave because there is no
possibility of regressing. The only possibility is to have
another experience of the lightning, and therein produce the passage again. You are shot out from non-
language, without belonging. One can never belong
because it orbits. Because it's in permanent flight.
Like the moon that permanently falls. You cannot
catch it.

a word is a journey to
a non-word and back
again

non-language is a
falling moon

~

I was impatient when Patricia described a step or a
figure in tango. The words floated by, meaningless, ir-
relevant. The only measure of my learning would be
what I could do with my body. The only explanation
for dancing was dancing. I had to practise each step a
thousand times until it came from muscle memory,
not from mental memory. I had to train my arms, legs,
and back into new patterns and overcome old habits.

I tried to walk as though I had never walked before, believing that if I could wipe the slate clean then I could write a more honest phrase overtop of it. I considered my body one muscle at a time so that I experienced my weight from my knees or from my hips or from my back, the flex and pull and stride.

Deja de pensar, Patricia smiled.

And another thing, she said. Breathe.

You are still too stiff, she told me one day. Here and here.

She touched her back and her shoulders.

Try this.

She tied her scarf around my head, covering my eyes.

Okay?

The soft pressure on my head was comforting. It was good to have an excuse to close my eyes, but the blindness was harder to accept. Patricia put one hand on each of my shoulders, facing me.

Now walk, she said.

I stepped into the darkness. I could feel the weight of her hands, enough to know she was there but not enough to stop me. There was resistance, then the darkness opened.

Keep walking, she said. Her voice came from far away. I held a map of the room in my mind. When I reached what I thought was the corner I hesitated.

I won't let you hit anything, she said.

Patricia turned. I followed, striding into nothingness. My toes bent when I pushed forward. The sway of my body was subtler now. I floated through an invisible groove in the air, using the sides of an imagined space for balance. For one step I was perfectly aligned with strength and lightness. My body was a single force, a single weight. Patricia's hands were no longer against my shoulders but somehow a part of them. I must have smiled from under the blindfold.

You can feel it, no? she said.

My ankles wobbled, sending tremors up my legs through my knees. She put her hands on my shoulders.

I breathed. We walked.

Fine, said Patricia. Now this.

She put one hand on the centre of my chest.

Again, walk, she said, but walk through me.

Her weight was stronger this time, and because there was only one place where we touched I had to lead with the direction of my torso. My shoulders were wings. They turned when I walked, one shoulder back as the opposite leg moved forward, swinging on the pivot at the centre of my body where the palm of Patricia's hand was hard against me.

Blind and without music, I walked around the room, striding into the future. I could hear our breath and the sound of our shoes on the tiles. I had the feeling of falling. I wondered if Patricia would kiss me, then I realized that I wished she would.

~

So language is not a point, but a passage, I said.

A passage, a translation, an exile, said Vanesa. Because I also believe that an intense experience of creativity can exile us from ourselves. An internal exile. It's like your own voice has run away. Because the anterior voice has to arrive. One receives one's experience of who they could have been without knowing it, and here I return to what you signalled at the beginning, that it's an un-knowing related to the unknowing of forgetting. Because in reality we forget how those primary experiences were.

creativity is an internal exile

a voice is an animal living in time

Because maybe you have the luck to remember something that you lived when you had three years of age, she continued, but in the moment that you tell it, you change the reality.

age is a possession

From that memory you're going to translate yourself, she said, and with that you're going to betray yourself. Because the categories with which you remember are categories, posterior.

translation is betrayal

Each word is a unique category, I echoed. Does the experience keep living, or is it changed by naming it?

writing is murder

Ah, how terrible! said Vanesa. Yes. At times we kill things, you see? There are things that one doesn't write in order not to kill them. It's preferable that they continue to orbit around us.

She told me about how she had heard some writers say, "My best book has not been written" and how at first she hadn't known what they meant. Then one day she understood: what they should have added, she said, is that their best book had not been written … nor would they ever write it.

Because there's an existence there, she explained, and a happiness for something that, if it isn't lowered to words, lives. And if it is lowered to words, it might not be found, or it destroys that life.

It makes me think of the sadness that we mentioned before, I said. Each time we write, we are killing an experience that's purer than the words that we're using to call it. And from there comes the sadness of consciousness. You used the word, "to lower" into language. As if the experience were up high, and words were down below it …

It's more dense, the word, Vanesa nodded. It has a density.

~

The burnt frame of an old car hulked in front of the door to Patricia's apartment, blackened with ashes, the back seat scattered with newspapers.

I'll just finish this, Patricia called down from the rooftop, gesturing with a cigarette that was dwarfed by stars.

We hailed a taxi and drove through La Boca to the *milonga*, the weekly tango event that Patricia had selected for that night. We were far from the streets that had been painted with bright primary colours where dozens of police officers wandered during the day to ensure that tourists felt safe. All the alleys were empty. Big chunks of cement were lit with dull light and a few puddles sprawled between the pavement and the sidewalk like bodies. At first naively, then with shame, I thought the streets looked like stages where a door would open and someone would start singing, looking up at the stars that were really the lights of a theatre – shame because I knew nothing of what it was like to live there.

We stopped at a gate where a single bulb shone through white bars. I was between two worlds, both of them safe and therefore familiar, the taxi on one side which could drive away from all of this, and the *milonga* on the other side of the gate, brightly lit and full of people, while down the road in either direction night extended toward an unknown truth that I would never discover because if I did, I assumed, it would be among the last things I learned. I imagined walking away in the direction of the departing taxi, fading into the dark between the low cement houses, walking as though naked in the world, having given up so that I could fade into the city, disappear. I wished for a spiritual submission that didn't require violence. I wanted to give up, to open, without being hurt.

The *milonga* had been held in the same hall on the same night of the week for eighty years. It also seemed that eighty was the average age of the dancers. Patricia, at fifty-two, was like a daughter to many of them. She kissed them on the cheek like someone coming home from the city to a place where everyone was family. I was a child, a lucky child, at the same time that I was proud to be the smiling young man beside her. We found a table and ate *empanadas* and shared a bottle of wine with ice cubes in our glasses so it lasted longer. Her friend Adolfo ate and drank with us. He worked as a light technician on movie sets and massaged his palms as if there were an ache deep in his bones that he was trying to work out through his fingertips. When he danced with Patricia his bones still carried that heaviness but he had found a way to transform it into sensuous strength.

Although Patricia had invited me there to watch, to see what a real *milonga* was like, she danced with me once. It didn't seem like the kind of place where I would ask anyone else. They had all arrived in couples, looking as though they had been married for fifty years, and it was not a beginners' crowd. I kept my movements simple, re-enacting the most basic values of what I had learned, knowing that it was better to be reliably modest than a spectacular disaster. Regardless, my hands were sweaty and I couldn't find my knees. In spite of the massive hall there was always someone in my way. I could feel their eyes on me.

Forget everything and just enjoy the music, Patricia whispered in my ear.

When we had circled the floor and were once more in front of our table, Adolfo winked and gave me the thumbs up.

Otherwise I watched the elderly. I watched how they danced, first their feet and then, when I understood where the dance was really happening, their torsos, trying to find the moment when they turned. But mostly I watched how the dance kept them together, how they had been married this long because they held each other at least once a week in a room full of friends. Nobody talked. Nobody even looked up. The men gazed into the infinite sadness of the floor, finding there a weary attention that allowed them to turn inward to their bodies. The women's eyes looked far away, longing for a time and a body they could feel but couldn't see. At other moments their eyes were downcast, even closed, as if each woman had found a way to join her partner by following his dreams. Somewhere Ernesto Sábato had written, "Only gringos dance tango for fun."

Could that expression be learned? Or was it the composition of a face I would never have? I remembered Silvia telling me, We don't have your face here, meaning that the ancestors of my face had not settled in Buenos Aires. My head was too round, lacking angles. My face was soft. But later, when a few weeks had passed, she said, You don't look like you're from here, but your gestures are.

Maybe you lived here in a past life, she concluded.

Patricia danced with Adolfo and with others while I watched and grew sleepy. At three o'clock in the morning we left with another couple who offered to give us a ride. Through the window of the car the streets of La Boca seemed even more mysterious than before, the curtain left open on a stage where all the actors dozed in the wings.

We turned west toward Constitución. The backs of two men walking in the middle of the road lit up in the headlights. Where were they going at this time of night? Where were *we* going? Neither one of the men looked back. They folded to the side, parting, one to the right and one to the left. We slipped between them. I thought of their homes. This was their street, their night.

Patricia complained that the *cortinas*, the transition songs or "curtains," between the *tandas*, the sets of three tangos, were too long and they were bringing down the *milonga*. The DJ was no good and everything was getting worse. And what about this road, *che*, it was terrible. The car became a bubble of laughter floating through the night. Dancing together had transformed us into shimmering globes of metallic light, like mercury.

~

Do you use the word "creative" or "creativity"? I asked. How do you feel with that word?

If I think of the act of creativity, said Vanesa, the result is difficult for me to apply. To create is like … I don't know. The word is used, but I realize that I don't use it.

Instead, she preferred the word "*re*create."

It is like a cousin of creativity, she said. It isn't an act of once-and-for-all, but it's an act that relaunches all the time.

What is it that limits you most in writing?

There are many limits, she said. And if I respond to it easily, and in one mode not very truthfully, or with a minor truth, it would be a lack of time. But more than that, when I'm working on writing I'm a little crazy. I'm not centred. Not at all. I start to live in two times, and those two times are very strong.

This is the last question, I said. How do you react in front of work that doesn't please you?

I suffer when it pleases me, when it pleases me and I know that none of the editors of this country are going to like it. In the face of that circumstance, I continue ahead because I can't avoid it. I will edit it myself, that possibility always exists … a rubber stamp editorial lifeboat among friends. When something I'm writing doesn't please me, I give it some time. And if in that time it doesn't go, it is because it doesn't go.

And how do you know? I asked.

Because it's like love, she said. If nothing happens to you, it doesn't go. Literature in me is absolutely passionate and loving, further than what I can tell you.[11]

I walked Vanesa home from the bar. She said she would invite me up for coffee, just as Mariana had said of a place where creativity was not only something one makes but a way of sharing life with people, but she saw patients from ten o'clock until midnight and had to prepare. When I explained the emphasis of my project, she nodded and said, Yes, *Estamos totalmente construidos por metáforas.* We are totally constructed by metaphors.

I walked away into a night that was bursting with hope. Words went out on their eternal departure, flinging toward the unnameable possibilities that orbited around the cluster of my being. Not even around my self, for that was too singular, too discrete. As they got closer to the place that I had strained to throw

creativity is a spinning top

creativity is movement

creativity is love

them, the words dissolved into liquid particles that broke apart like sunlight through falling water. Word after word flew beyond what language could do into a bright crack in the universe where all I heard was the sound that lips make when they smile. Then everything went quiet except for the hum of being alive.

~

The next lesson did not go well. None of my limbs fit together and the ones that did felt as if they were tied with bits of old twine. My legs flapped below the knees and my arms had no strength in them no matter how much I tugged at their weight. I shouted at my body from my brain – Turn left! Strong back! Lead from your chest! – but all my words were drowned out by a tight grinding sound that came from my teeth. With sharp sighs and annoyed grunts, I tried to show that I was disappointed in my performance so that Patricia wouldn't have to say it herself. We finished early.

Everyone has days when they can't dance, said Patricia. The problem is when you let it get you down.

There could be days when the opposite happened, she said, when life was terrible and dance could lift you as though there were nothing else in the world but tango. I told her about the years I had lived in Montreal, where I had danced nearly three times a week, although not tango. I could feel her listening.

There was another reason I was upset. The more I thought about it the more certain I became that she could see it in my eyes even though I wasn't saying it. Something inside was breaking. I wanted it to break, but it wouldn't. Ask me what's wrong, I begged without words, knowing that I would never tell her because it didn't make sense until I was walking home and it hit fully, landing into language that contorted and pulled away from the feeling as if they didn't quite fit together, as if there were more to say or maybe less. I felt better but I still wanted to cry. I needed the dance even though it was hard. The saddest thing I ever learned from tango was that I wasn't used to having another body close to mine.

Melancholy struck me then. It could have been because I was leaving soon. The city seemed to be turning its back. I didn't have a home there and maybe I never would. My feet hurt from walking. I told Patricia that I felt isolated. I didn't want to make a big deal out of it because I knew that it wasn't a grave affliction. It would pass. Loneliness was at times an integral part of the emotional landscape of Buenos Aires. Maybe everyone had to move through that stage of existential solitude to belong there. Maybe belonging meant feeling waves of loneliness undulating between the waves of nostalgia, lust, and dreams. When the Spanish philosopher José Ortega y Gasset (1883–1955) visited the city in the 1940s, he noted that "Argentine *tristeza* has a power that is so elementary, and massive, that it at once conquers any sensitive newcomer; I know of many who at first harboured thoughts of suicide for a whole week."[12] Maybe sadness was simply another form to fill out in an application for citizenship at the bottom of the world.

Nine days out of ten I was happy, I told Patricia, I was content – *contento*, a word I liked because it was imbued with happiness, too, and not just contentment – but then that one day hit and I forgot about all the other nine. That one day took over and I thought, I have nothing. It was worse than not knowing why I was there. I couldn't remember *if* I was there. All the reasons I had leading up to that moment were gone. There was just a wide, empty void. I could hardly tell if I were walking or standing still. It made no difference. I tried to figure out what brought it on, if there was something that happened to make me feel that way, but that was the problem. Nothing had happened. I had simply woken up in the void. Maybe it was because I didn't want to leave but it was not just that. It was inexplicable. And yet the only thing that made it pass was saying it.

Patricia's mouth was half-open in a way that, if photographed, would have made her look as if she were smiling. I noticed then that her gums were black and her teeth were stained from smoking. Her eyes were bloodshot. The curtain of her fatigue had blown aside and rough, honest care came through her in the way she listened.

She knew what I was saying before I finished saying it.

Chico, I'm like that, too, she said. Next time, don't be lonely. Just call me and we'll eat something. It's that simple.

~

There were other interviews. I met writers in cafés and bars all over the city.

I talked with crime writer Leonardo Oyola (1973–) about his tattoos, and how, during a difficult time when he had no work, he had separated from his girlfriend, and his son had just been born, he had visited a tattoo artist and mentioned the novel he was trying to write. The tattoo artist asked what was the title of the novel. *Chamamé,* Leonardo had said, the name of a kind of folk music from the north of Argentina. The tattoo artist proposed to write it across his chest so that every time he woke up and saw it in the mirror he would feel the pressure to write, to justify what was there. Leonardo agreed, even though he regretted how big it was. The novel won the 2008 Hammet Prize for best crime novel written in Spanish.

The tattoo worked, he said. It made me write.

That afternoon in Almagro, over beers and peanuts, Leonardo told me that there was no objective way to read.

We all read subjectively, he said. We read a book in agreement with our experiences, our previous reading. Everything cultural affects us. What tattoos and literature have in common is that they both remain.

Then he laughed.

That's also why I started giving my novels short titles, because if not it costs a lot and hurts a lot.

And the older you are, the more it hurts, he added, suddenly sombre.

I wondered if it was the same for writing. Starting out seemed painful enough. But there was beauty in the way he and his wife wrote side by side.

My wife is a writer, he explained, and we both write at night. The pact that we have is that we always go to bed at the same time. If one of us is writing and the other isn't, we have to hold on until the other finishes, even if it goes until seven in the morning. There are stages in which we are both writing and they are pretty moments because we sleep and wake up together, talking about our characters or situations as if we're talking about a familiar friend. And that's what happened during the last five novels that I wrote with her, I noticed how the characters doubled, became corporeal, how they had life. I said to myself, this is going to work.

So it was possible, I thought, to share a writing life.

Every novel is a daughter of the moment in which you write it, said Leonardo.

And there were more conversations.

I talked to novelist and short-story writer Oliverio Coelho (1977–), one of *Granta* magazine's top 40 under 40 Latin American Writers and winner of the Edmundo Valades Latin American Prize in Mexico and the National Initiation Prize in Argentina. He told me about writing and training, how the blog he kept was similar to the way soccer players train and sometimes don't finish the game; in training they can do things with more freedom, things that in the moment are beautiful but don't always end in a goal.

There are writers who don't train, he said, and this influences the quality of what they do. But if it doesn't entertain you then there's no point in doing it. It's like painters with their sketches. Not all sketches are going to become paintings, but the artist enjoys those sketches because they have no destination. They're pure freedom.

There was something curious about the soccer metaphor.

The formation of the team, Oliverio explained, the system of the game they have, is related to the team's identity. A writer finds his or her identity in the tone. There are writers with very potent language, but if they don't find the tone they can slip. They are scribes, but not writers.

It's interesting, I said, because the writer is singular. He or she works alone. But you're describing a team.

Yes, a team can be thought of as a unity.

The writer as a team.

When I asked him how he knew when a story was working, Oliverio switched to a mechanical metaphor.

Because there's a click that resolves the situation of paralysis in the narration, he said. It's not a paralysis in the writing, but in the narration. The click can happen after drinking a whisky or throwing yourself in bed to read, or before falling asleep, which is the worst because you can't ignore it even though you don't want to get out of bed. I always think I'll remember it tomorrow, but the next day I remember nothing.

One makes one's own rules, Oliverio added. But in order for those rules to function, one must have a strategy. The rules don't exist a priori. They're verified in the practice.

They come out of the office, I reflected, perennially enchanted by the word *oficio*, which had office, practice, and work folded into its meaning.

Right. In chess and in soccer the rules exist a priori, said Oliverio.

So each story needed to establish and adhere to its own rules. It had to be internally coherent. And that coherence could not be lent to another work without succumbing to what Oliverio called the novel-script. Again, each work broke away from the past to find its place in a unique present. Each work lives alone, I thought. Part and apart.

More conversations.

I met Mercedes Araujo (1972–), poet and novelist, winner of the 2011 First Prize in the novel category from the Fondo National de las Artes (National Arts Fund of Argentina), to talk about the connection between her work as a lawyer and her work as a writer. I wanted to know more about the laws of fiction.

In the moment of writing, she said, I arrive mostly without pre-established resources, from a place of much intuition, and almost with the sensation of having no resources at all, until I can create the possibility, the resource, the gadget or contraption that will serve me for the particular creative process itself. But I can't call it a law, precisely because it lacks that possibility of being applicable in a general way to all creative processes.

So they're not rules either, I said, but they're things that come from the act of writing? Or are they there when you start? How do they appear?

There are distinct moments in writing, Mercedes said. One of those moments is like writing outside of the text, outside of language even, which is an internal writing, mental, which is like a quantity of sediment that revolves around something that's producing in you a certain disquiet.

I heard echoes of my conversation with Vanesa, the non-language source of being in the world.

This half-state of creation, Mercedes continued, hasn't been translated yet into any register. It's a very pleasant state because it's like a discovery, or complete freedom, that the body, the head, the intuition, the distinct forms we have with which to perceive, including reason, generate this sediment. It has to do with emotions, with fears, happiness, aesthetic registers, that the world gives you. Then after comes the challenge of tipping that over into language, if one works as a writer. And in that instance of tipping it over into language a species of impossibility appears, because not everything is really nameable. Language has its limits. There you enter into a situation in which one must accept that the material, which is language, has that physical limitation, as if it were a piece of wood. The big challenge is to see all the possibilities of speaking or not speaking.

More conversations. The city was breaking with metaphor.

~

I gave up on becoming the dancer I had longed to be. I was too stiff. There was too much to think about. I would never know the sublime pleasure of walking with dignity, well dressed, across the floor of a *milonga* to lift a woman into my embrace and glide across our regulated lust together. I would go back to flailing alone at folk festivals.

My last lesson ended and we changed out of our dance shoes. Patricia said she would come to Canada one day. She had heard there was good tango in Montreal. Maybe she could teach there. If not, then France – she had some French students who wanted her to start a tango school with them. She said it without any twinkle of hope in her eye, barely a breath of excitement in her voice. We walked up the stairs into the empty café, said goodnight to the owner as he mopped the floor, and stepped through the tiny door into the street. At the corner, Patricia put down her backpack and lit a cigarette and said, Wait for me.

She didn't say anything else, just inhaled and looked up at the tops of the buildings where they met the black shadow of the sky. The silence was so comfortable I was surprised when it was my own voice that broke it.

What will I find if I come back here in six months? I said.

Patricia didn't reply right away.

Una mierda, she said finally. *Una mierda*, she said again, louder, *Este país es una mierda*. This country is shit.

She swore and laughed and apologized for swearing, and when I made noises that said, It's fine, say whatever you need to say, she kept swearing and didn't laugh until she had finished.

This country is falling apart again, she said, and I want to leave. I am fifty-two years old and I have been working since I was fifteen. Why can't I save some money and have a good life?

She tilted her foot and looked at the bottom of her shoe. She was wearing thin green eyeliner that was the same colour of green that Pablo Neruda had used to write all of his poems.

In six months? she said. We'll still be here. It will have deterio-
rated but it won't have collapsed by then, not yet. One thing we
have as Argentine people is that we are very elastic. You have to be.

I realized then the audacity of my eagerness to belong. I could
be *in* Buenos Aires, I could even be *with* Buenos Aires, but I would
never be *of* Buenos Aires.

She crushed her cigarette and her face lit up with the expression
that I recognized as hers but couldn't name until that moment. It
was the look of endurance. She hugged me and kissed me on the
cheek.

Sos un buen chico, she laughed. You're a good kid. Let me know
when you come back.

~

I climbed to the top floor of the National Library and rested in a
big chair with a view of the city. I read, then closed my book and
looked over the rooftops. When I descended through the stairwell,
having no patience for the elevator with its slow doors, there was
something hollow about the building, abandoned and lonely, as
though I were already far away.

That afternoon I walked to San Telmo and waited on a bench in
Parque Lezama until the time I had been told, then knocked on
the door of the apartment where I would conduct my final interview. We talked for two hours. When it was finished, the woman I
had been interviewing said she had forgotten that she was with
someone who wasn't speaking his first language.

It seems that you are at home, she said.

Something larger than our conversation closed around me. The
process of interviewing was now familiar. I knew how to take my
place, host the conversation, attend. Not that I had mastered my
role, but I recognized the patterns of experience. My time with the
question that had brought me to Buenos Aires was ending.

But what had I learned? The word "creativity" had become so
diluted that I wasn't sure it meant anything at all. I thought again

of Walter Benjamin. What he wrote about memory was just as true for metaphor: "He who has once begun to open the fan of memory never comes to the end of its segments; no image satisfies him, for he has seen that it can be unfolded, and only in its folds does the truth reside."[13]

I remembered something Oliverio Coelho had said in our conversation: that the word creativity was vague, that it had a social circulation that was too simple. It had become banal through overuse, and its contents or its potency had been diminished.

The word was an empty vessel. Or was it a vessel so full that there was no room for me?

Yet, even if creativity, the word, had been drained of its utility, it marked something that mattered. I needed it. I needed a way out of the world as it was. Through that way out, I would find my way back in.

For what I really wanted to know was whether I was a creative person. Each time I made something, writing, drawing, I found that it had been done much better before by someone else. My work emulated that of those I admired but it didn't make anything new. I hadn't set off on my own: I had gone to Buenos Aires, city of a million artists, in the footsteps of countless foreigners who had projected their dreams onto a place they barely knew. Wherever I went I recycled those dreams, variations on nostalgia, melancholy, and hope. I could hear my own echoes. There was no making. What little I did make was an imitation of lived experience.

If there were a world apart from language, as Mercedes and Vanesa had said, and it was rich and playful and sublime, why bring it into words at all? Why sully it with language that would only fail to do it justice? The creative act, ironically, destroyed while it made. Perhaps it was best avoided. And yet Mercedes and Vanesa kept writing. And Guillermo Martínez and Mariana Docampo and Juan Diego Incardona and Leonardo Oyola and Oliverio Coelho, they all kept writing.

What's most pressing is the desire, Mercedes had said. That I must go toward the creation of writing. To the action of writing.

And when I arrive there, to that place, the investigation continues, the question, the speculation.

I had been looking for the wrong thing the whole time. Creativity was not a quality or a process. It was not a commodity, it was not a fuel.

There was a short story by Julio Cortázar called "Carta a una Señorita en París" (Letter to a Young Lady in Paris) which described a man with the mysterious habit of vomiting up rabbits. The character's behaviour was awkward, but not apologetic. He spent the story devising ways to keep the rabbits hidden in the study while taking care of a friend's apartment. He saw "no reason for one to blush and isolate one's self and to walk around keeping one's mouth shut," but there were simple practical considerations, like how to keep the rabbits from nibbling at the books on the shelf.[14] It was a specific, unique metaphor for creativity. The work came unbidden, usually when the narrator was alone, and it was hard to conceal. It implied that creativity was involuntary divulgence. Creativity was vomiting rabbits. And even if none of them survived, the compulsion went on.

This was the nature of creativity that I had overlooked. "Being creative" was not something one set out to do. As cliché as it was to say it, creativity was not a destination, but a journey. The reason I had gone to Buenos Aires, to interview writers about their creative process, was only the excuse for the life that happened around those encounters. If anything, creativity was metabolism. One lived with it. One lived *by* it. It was a necessary way of being in the world, the only way. Not an idea but an action. Not a thing but a doing. Not a noun but a verb. The work itself – the story, the drawing, this very book – was no more than what was left over after living with a question.

~

My last days in Buenos Aires condensed and blurred. The buildings, the cars, the people, and the streets were vague and uncertain, as if they could vanish at any moment. I noticed more backs than faces and the sidewalks were charged with haste. Sounds blended together. I couldn't tell the difference between a voice and the clop of shoes. Colours softened, as though a grey silty powder had been rubbed over all my memories.

The city of my dreams no longer seemed intended for me. Until then I had thought that Buenos Aires and I were leaning in to one another, but in the end I was leaning alone. I would pine for my memories of the place, for my hopes of what it could have been, while the city would go on indifferent to whether I was there or not. It had presented a way of being that I wanted more of, shown what was possible with art, offered friendship and a home. And when I left it would do the same for someone else.

The sky was cool and grey on my last full day. I went for a walk with Gloria, who helped me choose a pair of shoes from the market in El Once because I had worn through the soles of the shoes I had brought. On the way home we stopped at Café de los Angelitos on Rivadavia where the ceilings were so high there really was room for angels. We talked about the things we hoped to write and about the house she planned to build with her boyfriend in Nicaragua. I told her that I was outside of love. Apart from it, not part of it. I blinked away tears.

Leave a little door open in your heart, she said. Leave a little door open for love, Adrián.

We asked for the bill. Outside it was finally raining.

Gloria had work to do until dinnertime so I went for another long walk, this time to Avenida Santa Fe, looking for a book that I hoped to give to Isabel at the radio station. The streets were wet and black. I walked without an umbrella. Everything was dissolving, as though the city were made of cardboard. I couldn't find the book I wanted but I found a different one instead.

I met Gloria again for dinner at midnight. The entrance to the *parilla* is still clear when I think of it, the brick step at the corner of the street and the white iron bars on the door. Gloria asked if they were open and a man with an apron said yes. We agreed on a table by the window where the curtains were drawn. I remember the paper placemats and the yellow label on the bottle of wine and how both of us were tired. We talked about the most difficult times in our lives, the times that we now drew strength from because we had gotten through them. I was grateful that we had known each other for so many years and had found ourselves at this table in this city. Then all too soon I was gone.

Afterword: Critical Metaphor Literacy and the Meanings of Creativity

This book was the residue of a question, "What does it mean to be creative?" It manifested a practice I have called Critical Metaphor Literacy – learning to read the personal and social significance of phenomena by the metaphors used to narrate experience, and generating new metaphors that expand possibilities for thinking otherwise.[1] Beyond the direct discussion of metaphors for creativity, each narrative vignette entailed a hidden metaphor of its own: the account of searching the city for books on the reading list for the seminar teased the idea that *creativity is a scavenger hunt*. The scene of visiting a Sanskrit chanting group suggested that *creativity is meditation*. The surreal experience of stopping by Bar de Roberto to hear a tango singer late at night imagined that *creativity is a dream*, and more. Each untitled scene invited a conversation about hidden and explicit metaphor, some directly related to creativity and others not. They were unnamed so as to expand in possibility, with the goal of multiplying ways of knowing and opening, not closing, new meanings. Some metaphors were more useful than others. Many contradicted. Many were obscure. But by exploring a range, it was possible to sense the complexity of what it means to write.

The purpose of collecting and narrating metaphors of creativity was twofold: first, to show how any idea could be developed, nuanced, and brought to life by exploring the lived experience of the metaphors around it, and second, to emphasize the necessary incompleteness of greater understanding. The compendium, after all, would never be finished. If the reader has felt inspired to consider metaphors that are not included here, then this book has done its work. It is up to the imaginative engagement of the questioner to find likenesses between separate entities and create something new by carrying one meaning across to the other. Making metaphor is a fundamental creative act. It is as common as a thought.

The episodic structure was a reflection of the jotted notes that were the first written incarnation of my question, and an acknowledgement of the kaleidoscopic nature of memory. Scenes overlapped, fell away, imagined, interpreted, retraced, and erased. Fragments made room for the things I didn't know. There was space between the events and the ideas. I was inspired by German cultural theorist and literary critic Walter Benjamin, his *One-way Street*, his *Archive*, his *Berlin Childhood around 1900*, and *The Arcades Project*. I had secretly always wished that Benjamin combined the structure of *One-way Street*, a compilation of aphorisms and insights into daily expressions of modernism, with "A Berlin Chronicle," which conjured tender and subtle moods through memoirs of youth. Here I sought to carry one across to the other, bringing the memoir to the fragments to make something new.

The meaningfulness of the fragments arose as much from their context as from their content, how they were situated among other fragments. Scenes from the interviews informed and nuanced the narrator's understandings of prose writing and calibrated the insights earned through exploration of a city. The juxtaposition of fragments suggested that the site of meaning was often between objects of focus, in the periphery. In the space between the stories, there was room for the wisdom of absence and forgetting. I hoped that the episodic structure would help the reader make connections of his or her own, exploring patterns and meanings beyond the ones I saw. A network emerged: metaphors for creativity were contextualized by the narratives that hosted them, and those narratives in turn were contextualized by the fragments and interview excerpts that surrounded them. The reflections made an incomplete whole, held together around the silence of things unsaid, unmade, not yet created. In the interval, carrying one meaning to another was the creative act of metaphor making.[2]

Translation was key. It was a metaphor for what happened between two identities in metaphor making itself (A = B), where one language was reflected by another, becoming something new in the process. I wanted to keep some parts of the interview transcripts deliberately awkward. If I had made the speech smoother in translation, changing the way we spoke in Spanish into how we would have spoken in English, some of the poetry of those conversations would be lost. I wanted to *use words wrongly*, as Vanesa Guerra said. It was a way of breaking language to see what else might be inside it, beyond it, through it. More importantly, though, I wanted the conversations to sound uniquely Spanish. I had to show that the English version wasn't there to supplant the original, but was a variation on it. Even the Spanish transcript, typed out from recordings of the interviews, was a variation on the event that happened in time and space between two living people. And, if Vanesa Guerra's comments were taken to heart, then even that conversation was only a variation on a non-language experience of existence that we both brought into words for the convenience of exchange and contact. Somewhere that wasn't a place, sometime that wasn't before or after, there was an immutable source that eschewed language. Every representation was another possibility.

There was another kind of translation in the act of remembering, which carried experience from past to present and transformed it along the way. Remembrance, as Benjamin wrote, was "the capacity for endless interpolations into what has been."[3] The number of possibilities offered by memory wasn't limited by the length of the time of the remembered event. Each moment could be revisited, reconsidered, and examined through multiple visions. It became a reflection of my relation to time as much as a record of experience.[4]

Critical Metaphor Literacy began as an idea and became a practice. The same method of survey, examination, and generation could be taken up in efforts to understand the meaningfulness of concepts like government, authority, community, God, death, love, and more. The questioner begins with a search for different views on his or her subject of interest, paying close attention to the metaphors that are implicit or explicit in each perspective. Living practitioners are consulted, people who have engaged earnestly with the phenomenon that the questioner wants to understand, always with an eye for invitations to think otherwise. What does this word mean to you? What does it mean to me? Tell me a story about that. Finally, the questioner composes narrative accounts of the lived encounters, situating the question in personal experience and demonstrating how insight comes from sensitivity to context. The results will vary – they *must* vary – depending on the particular experience of the questioner. Trying out this method in different languages, in different places, and with different topics, is an invitation to consider the meaningfulness of a subject and the questioner's relation to it. With practice, metaphors become more apparent. Daily speech takes on new life.

While writing this book, I was reading a lot of Clarice Lispector, Roberto Bolaño, and Walter Benjamin.[5] The stories told here would have come out differently if I had been concurrently reading other works or if I were inspired by other voices. Just as these stories changed each time they were incarnated through writing, first in the scraps of notes while I wandered in Buenos Aires, then in the journal when I returned to Eugenio's home in the evenings, then months and even years later in this book, so would a subsequent version be altered by the whimsy of memory, experience, inspiration, hope, and circumstance. Personal writing exists in community and in time. In Bateson's words, it "affirms relationship, for it includes these implied warnings: this is what I think at this moment, this is what I remember now, continuing to grow and change."[6] These stories will change as I change.

Critical Metaphor Literacy envisions research and education as the dynamic and ongoing search for further possibilities for understanding. Instead of viewing curriculum as a predetermined set of learning outcomes, it is embodied here as a creative and infinite examination of experience and language. As with William Pinar's[7] distinction between curriculum (in many ways, a fixed object) and *currere* (from the Latin, literally "running of the course"), I am more interested in metaphor's potential as a verb than in its properties as a noun. Through the reflective practice of metaphor making, words become worlds anew.

Acknowledgments

A friend once asked if I felt lonely when I write. It is such solitary work, after all. The truth is, writing is a communion with people, all people, for language is born of those who use it. I hear them when I write. I think of them, and they are with me.

I am indebted to the writers I met in Buenos Aires, Argentina, who generously shared their time, thoughts, and work. I continue to be inspired by their commitment to a life of letters. They are Guillermo Martínez, Mariana Docampo, Juan Diego Incardona, Vanesa Guerra, Oliverio Coelho, Mercedes Araujo, Pablo Katchadjian, Matías Capelli, Leonardo Oyola, Ignacio Copani, and Javier van de Couter. I am especially thankful to Gloria Carrión Fonseca, Mercedes Pagalday, and Carolina Orloff for their care, guidance, and companionship, and to Eugenio Francisco Gastiazoro, who gave me a home away from home. Thank you also to Patricia, Silvia, and Sabina for all the walks, with music or without.

This book began at the Centre for Cross-Faculty Inquiry in Education at the University of British Columbia, under the sage guidance of Carl Leggo, Norman Amundson, and Anthony Clarke. During that time, William Pinar and Erika Hasebe-Ludt also became important mentors to whom I still turn for inspiration and council. Much of this book was written and revised while I was a visiting post-doctoral fellow at Teachers College, Columbia University, where I was fortunate to work with Janet Miller.

Research was generously supported by the Social Sciences and Humanities Research Council of Canada, the Liu Institute for Global Issues, and the University of British Columbia.

At McGill-Queen's University Press, I am grateful to Jonathan Crago, Mark Abley, Curtis Fahey, and the anonymous reviewers for their thoughtful comments. This book was profoundly improved by their wisdom, insight, and attention.

Long journeys are fuelled by friendship. Thank you to Sean Mills, Peter Dietz, Samantha Green, Robert Kotyk, Chu-Lynne Ng, David Peters, Meaghan Jones, Mali Bain, Amber Blenkiron, Amanda Mitchell, and Liliane Ehrhart, whose support I depended on to write and revise this work, but more importantly to share in the pedestrian joy of days well lived. Thank you to Gary Lyons for teaching me how to draw and for inspiring me to look closer. Juan Pablo Vieytes and Shamsher Virk, let's camp again by a river under stars. I miss you guys. I guard a special gratitude for the United World Community.

Finally, I reserve the simplest sentences for love that is the greatest, since language will always fall short: thank you to my parents, Rob and Diana, and to my brother, Colin. Thank you for Quadra Island. Thank you for words and for silence.

Notes

INTRODUCTION

1 Singer, *Modes of Creativity*, 106; Weisberg, *Creativity*, 90.

2 Hemingway, *A Moveable Feast*, 13.

3 Bellingham, "A Phenomenological and Thematic Interpretation of the Experience of Creativity"; Funke, "On the Psychology of Creativity"; Miall, "Metaphor and Transformation"; Singer, *Modes of Creativity*; Weisberg, *Creativity*.

4 Filloux, "Steve Jobs."

5 Cortázar, *Hopscotch*, i.

6 Caistor, *Buenos Aires*, 82.

7 Wilson, *Buenos Aires*, 2.

8 Ibid.

9 Ibid., 3.

10 Wikipedia, "Argentine Literature."

11 Williams, "Argentina."

12 CADRA, "Ley del Fomento del Libro y la Lectura – Ley No. 25.446."

13 Romero, "Argentina's New Literary Tradition."

14 Nawotka, "Buenos Aires."

A PRELIMINARY SURVEY OF METAPHORS FOR CREATIVITY

1 In Wilson, *Buenos Aires*, 41.

2 Ibid.

3   Ibid., 35.

4   Ibid., 43.

5   Lubart, "Cross-cultural Perspectives on Creativity," 269.

6   Weisberg, *Creativity*.

7   Singer, *Modes of Creativity*, 106; Weisberg, *Creativity*, 90.

8   Plato, *The Portable Plato*.

9   Gaut, "The Philosophy of Creativity."

10 Aristotle, *Poetics*, 5.

11 Wilson, *Buenos Aires*, 33.

12 Bellingham, "A Phenomenological and Thematic Interpretation of the Experience of Creativity"; Hirsch, *The Demon and the Angel*.

13 Weisberg, *Creativity*.

14 Singer, *Modes of Creativity*.

15 Weisberg, *Creativity*.

16 Singer, *Modes of Creativity*, 52.

17 Bellingham, "A Phenomenological and Thematic Interpretation of the Experience of Creativity," 69.

18 Lorca, *Theory and Play of the Duende*.

19 Ibid.

20 In Bellingham, "A Phenomenological and Thematic Interpretation of the Experience of Creativity," 110.

21 Dillard, *The Writing Life*, 64.

22 Weisberg, *Creativity*.

23 See: Lumsden and Findlay, "Evolution of the Creative Mind"; Mumford and Mobley, "Creativity, Biology, and Culture"; Simonton, "Scientific Creativity as a Combinatorial Process" and "The Creative Imagination in Picasso's *Guernica* Sketches."

24 Gaut, "The Philosophy of Creativity"; Kozbelt, Beghetto, and Runco, "Theories of Creativity"; Weisberg, *Creativity*.

25 Kozbelt, Beghetto, and Runco, "Theories of Creativity."

26 William James in Moran, "Metaphor Foundations in Creativity Research."

27 See also Acar and Runco, "Thinking in Multiple Directions" and "Assessing Associative Distance among Ideas Elicited by Tests of

Divergent Thinking"; Kozbelt, Beghetto, and Runco, "Theories of Creativity."

28 Acar and Runco, "Assessing Associative Distance among Ideas Elicited by Tests of Divergent Thinking."

29 See Simonton, "Scientific Creativity as a Combinatorial Process," "The Creative Imagination in Picasso's *Guernica* Sketches," and "Quality and Purpose, Quantity and Chance."

30 Kozbelt, Beghetto, and Runco, "Theories of Creativity."

31 Gabora, "Why the Creative Process Is Not Darwinian."

32 Weisberg, *Creativity*.

33 Merrell, "Creation."

34 Ibid., 121.

35 Singer, *Modes of Creativity*, 66.

36 Ibid.

37 Merrell, "Creation."

38 Gaut, "The Philosophy of Creativity"; See also Lubart and Sternberg, "Creativity."

39 Hemingway, *A Moveable Feast*, 13.

40 Singer, *Modes of Creativity*, 49.

41 Bellingham, "A Phenomenological and Thematic Interpretation of the Experience of Creativity"; Funke, "On the Psychology of Creativity"; Miall, "Metaphor and Transformation"; Singer, *Modes of Creativity*; Weisberg, *Creativity*.

42 Bellingham, "A Phenomenological and Thematic Interpretation of the Experience of Creativity"; Kozbelt, Beghetto, and Runco, "Theories of Creativity"; Miall, "Metaphor and Transformation"; Wallas, *The Art of Thought*.

43 See Khandwalla, "An Exploratory Investigation of Divergent Thinking through Protocol Analysis"; Kozbelt, Beghetto, and Runco, "Theories of Creativity."

44 Filloux, "Steve Jobs."

45 Singer, *Modes of Creativity*, 67.

46 Miall, "Metaphor and Transformation."

47 Kozbelt, Beghetto, and Runco, "Theories of Creativity."

48 Bellingham, "A Phenomenological and Thematic Interpretation of the Experience of Creativity."

49 Weisberg, *Creativity*.

50 See Singer, *Modes of Creativity*.

51 Ibid.

52 Dorfman, *Heading South, Looking North*, 275.

53 Csikszentmihalyi, *Flow* and "Where Is the Evolving Milieu"; Meusburger, Funke, and Wunder, *Milieus of Creativity*, 3.

54 Meusburger, Funke, and Wunder, *Milieus of Creativity*.

55 Förster, "The Unconscious City," 219.

56 Sternberg, "Domain-generality vs. Domain-specificity of Creativity."

57 In Gaut, "The Philosophy of Creativity," 1035.

58 Singer, *Modes of Creativity*, 64.

59 Funke, "On the Psychology of Creativity."

60 Kaufman and Sternberg, *The Cambridge Handbook of Creativity*.

61 Florida, *Who's Your City?*

62 Moran, "Metaphor Foundations in Creativity Research."

63 Boden, "Conceptual Spaces."

64 Moran, "Metaphor Foundations in Creativity Research."

65 Ibid.

66 Ibid.

67 Kaufman and Baer, "The Amusement Park Theory of Creativity."

68 Ibid., 321.

69 Ibid.

70 In Wilson, *Buenos Aires*, vii.

71 Kaufman and Sternberg, *The Cambridge Handbook of Creativity*, 477; Weisberg, *Creativity*, 100.

72 See Aristotle, *Poetics*.

73 Sternberg, "Domain-generality vs. Domain-specificity of Creativity."

74 See also Rubenson, "Human Capital and the Matthew Effect" and "On Creativity, Economics, and Baseball."

75 Sábato, *On Heroes and Tombs*, 7.

76 Merrell, "Creation"; Miall, "Metaphor and Transformation."

77 Boden, "Conceptual Spaces"; Moran, "Metaphor Foundations in Creativity Research."

78 Perkins, in Moran, "Metaphor Foundations in Creativity Research," 1.

79 Ibid.

80 Singer, *Modes of Creativity*, 56.

81 Moran, "Metaphor Foundations in Creativity Research."

82 Nakamura and Csikszentmihalyi, "The Concept of Flow."

83 Perry, "Flow and the Art of Fiction."

84 Wilson, *Buenos Aires*, 43.

85 Bellingham, "A Phenomenological and Thematic Interpretation of the Experience of Creativity."

86 Ibid.

87 Ibid., 46.

88 Richards, "Everyday Creativity," 205.

89 Moran, "Metaphor Foundations in Creativity Research," 16.

THE METAPHOR METAPHOR

1 Cole, *Coyote and Raven Go Canoeing*; Hart, "Indigenous Worldviews, Knowledge, and Research."

2 Aristotle, *Poetics*.

3 Derrida, "White Mythology," 13.

4 Radman, *Metaphors*.

5 Derrida, "White Mythologies," 32.

6 Aristotle, *Poetics*, 47.

7 Manuel Goldman, in Radman, *Metaphors*, 38.

8 Kofman, *Nietzsche and Metaphor*.

9 Radman, *Metaphors*.

10 Kofman, *Nietzsche and Metaphor*; Pinker, *The Stuff of Thought*; Radman, *Metaphors*; Ricoeur, *The Rule of Metaphor*.

11 Goodman, in Radman, *Metaphors*, 148.

12 Derrida, "White Mythologies," 18.

13 Radman, *Metaphors*.

14 Derrida, "White Mythologies."

15 Lakoff and Johnson, *Metaphors We Live By*.

16 Ricoeur, *The Rule of Metaphor*, 18.

17 Miall, "Metaphor and Transformation"; Moran, "Metaphor Foundations in Creativity Research."

VARIATIONS ON A SURVEY OF METAPHORS FOR CREATIVITY

1 Benjamin, *The Arcades Project*, 456.

2 Bateson, *Peripheral Visions*, 5.

3 See Ruitenberg, "Distance and Defamiliarization."

4 Translation of a conversation recorded in La Tienda Del Café de Avenida Elcano y Conde, Buenos Aires, 11 July 2012.

5 Docampo, *La Fe*, 88.

6 Translation of a conversation recorded in Café Adaggio, Saavedra Park, Buenos Aires, 12 July 2012.

7 Incardona, *Rock Barrial*; *El Campito*; *Villa Celina*; *Objetos Maravillosos*.

8 Translation of a conversation recorded at a table in the garden, Espacio Cultural Nuestros Hijos, Buenos Aires, 17 July 2012.

9 Borges, *Ficciones*, 58.

10 Guerra, *La Sombra del Animal*, 47.

11 Translation of a conversation recorded at a bar on the corner of Calle Carranza and Calle Nicaragua, Palermo, Buenos Aires, 19 July 2012.

12 France, *Bad Times in Buenos Aires*, 100.

13 Benjamin, "A Berlin Chronicle," 6.

14 Cortázar, *Blow-up and Other Stories*, 37.

AFTERWORD

1 McKerracher, "Understanding Creativity, One Metaphor at a Time."

2 See Zwicky, "Mathematical Analogy and Metaphorical Insight"; *Wisdom & Metaphor*.

3 Benjamin, "A Berlin Chronicle," 16.

4 See Benjamin, "A Berlin Chronicle"; Woolf, "A Sketch of the Past."

5 Lispector, *Near to the Wild Heart*; *A Breath of Life*; *The Passion*

According to G.H.; The Hour of the Star; The Stream of Life. Bolaño,
The Third Reich; The Insufferable Gaucho; The Savage Detectives;
The Skating Rink; 2666; Amulet; Last Evenings on Earth. Benjamin,
"One-way Street"; "A Berlin Chronicle."

6 Bateson, *Peripheral Visions*, 76.
7 Pinar, *What Is Curriculum Theory?*

Bibliography

Acar, Selcuk, and Mark Runco. "Assessing Associative Distance among Ideas Elicited by Tests of Divergent Thinking." *Creativity Research Journal* 26 (2014): 229–38.

– "Thinking in Multiple Directions: Hyperspace Categories in Divergent Thinking." *Psychology of Aesthetics, Creativity, and the Arts* 9, no. 1 (2015): 41–53.

Amundson, Norman. *Metaphor Making: Your Career, Your Life, Your Way.* Richmond, BC: Ergon Communications 2010.

"Argentine Literature" [Wikipedia]. http://en.wikipedia.org/wiki/Argentine_literature.

Aristotle. *Poetics.* Translated by Kenneth McLeish. London: Nick Hern Books 1997.

Barnstone, Willis. *With Borges on an Ordinary Evening in Buenos Aires: A Memoir.* Chicago: University of Illinois Press 1993.

Bateson, Mary Catherine. *Peripheral Visions: Learning along the Way.* New York: HarperCollins 1994.

Bellingham, Robin. "A Phenomenological and Thematic Interpretation of the Experience of Creativity." MA thesis, Auckland University of Technology, 2008. http://www.academia.edu/25763164/Robin_Bellingham_A_phenomenological_and_thematic_interpretation_of_the_experience_of_creativity_2008_Faculty_of_Health_and_Environmental_Science.

Benjamin, Walter. *The Arcades Project.* Edited by Howard Eiland and Kevin McLaughlin. Cambridge, MA: Belknap Press of Harvard University Press 1999.

– *Berlin Childhood around 1900.* Translated by Howard Eiland. Cambridge, MA.: Belknap Press of Harvard University Press 2006.

– "A Berlin Chronicle." In *Reflections: Essays, Aphorisms, Autobiographical Writings.* New York: Schocken Books 2007.

– "One-way Street." In *One-way Street and Other Writings.* Translated by J.A. Underwood. Toronto: Penguin Books 2009.

– *Walter Benjamin's Archive: Images, Texts, Signs.* Edited by Ursula Marx et al. Translated by Esther Leslie. New York: Verso 2007.

Boden, Margaret. "Conceptual Spaces." In Peter Meusburger, Joachim Funke, and Edgar Wunder, eds., *Milieus of Creativity: An Interdisciplinary Approach to Spatiality of Creativity,* 235–45 Dordrecht, Netherlands: Springer 2009.

Bolaño, Roberto. *2666.* Translated by Natasha Wimmer. New York: Farrar, Straus and Giroux 2008.

– *Amulet.* Translated by Chris Andrews. New York: New Directions 2006.

– *The Insufferable Gaucho.* Translated by Chris Andrews. New York: New Directions 2010.

– *Last Evenings on Earth.* Translated by Chris Andrews. New York: New Directions 2006.

– *The Savage Detectives.* Translated by Natasha Wimmer. London: Picador 2009.

– *The Skating Rink.* Translated by Chris Andrews. New York: New Directions 2009.

– *The Third Reich.* Translated by Natasha Wimmer. Toronto: Penguin 2011.

Borges, Jorge Luis. *Ficciones.* Edited by Anthony Kerrigan. New York: Grove Press 1962.

– "On Metaphor." In *On Writing,* 42–6. Translated by Peter Robinson. New York: Penguin 2010.

CADRA. "Ley del Fomento del Libro y la Lectura – Ley No. 25.446." *Centro de Administración de Derechos Reprográficos Asociación Civil – Gestión Colectiva de Derechos de Autor* (n.d.). http://www.cadra.org.ar/upload/Ley_25446.pdf.

Caistor, Nick. *Buenos Aires: A Cultural Guide.* Northampton, MA: Interlink
Publishing Group 2015.

Catmull, Edwin, and Amy Wallace. *Creativity Inc: Overcoming the Unseen
Forces That Stand in the Way of True Inspiration.* Toronto: Random
House Canada 2014.

Cole, Peter. *Coyote and Raven Go Canoeing: Coming Home to the Village.*
Montreal and Kingston: McGill-Queen's University Press 2006.

Cortázar, Julio. *Blow-up and Other Stories.* Translated by Paul Blackburn.
New York: Collier Books 1963.

– *Hopscotch.* Translated by Gregory Rabassa. New York: Pantheon
Books 1966.

Csikszentmihalyi, Mihaly. *Flow: The Psychology of Optimal Experience.*
New York: Harper Collins Publishers 1990.

– "Where Is the Evolving Milieu? A Response to Gruber." *Creativity
Research Journal* 1 (1988): 60–2.

Derrida, Jacques. "White Mythology: Metaphor in the Text of Philosophy." *New Literary History* 6, no. 1 (1974): 5–74.

Dillard, Annie. *The Writing Life.* New York: Harper and Row 1989.

Docampo, Mariana. *La fe: Relatos.* Buenos Aires: Bajo la Luna 2011.

Dorfman, Ariel. *Heading South, Looking North: A Bilingual Journey.* New
York: Farrar, Straus, and Giroux 1998.

Estes, Zachary, and Thomas B. Ward. "The Emergence of Novel Attributes in Concept Modification." *Creativity Research Journal* 14, no. 2
(2002): 149–56.

Filloux, Frédéric. "Steve Jobs: Seven Lessons from Apple's Founder."
Guardian Newspaper Online, 10 October 2011.

Florida, Richard. *Who's Your City? How the Creative Economy Is Making
Where to Live the Most Important Decision of Your Life.* Toronto: Vintage
2009.

Förster, Jens. "The Unconscious City: How Expectancies about Creative
Milieus Influence Creative Performance." In Peter Meusburger,
Joachim Funke, and Edgar Wunder, eds., *Milieus of Creativity: An Interdisciplinary Approach to Spatiality of Creativity.* Dordrecht, Netherlands: Springer 2009. 219–35.

France, Miranda. *Bad Times in Buenos Aires: A Writer's Adventures in
Argentina.* Hopewell, NJ: Ecco Press 1998.

Funke, Joachim. "On the Psychology of Creativity." In Peter Meusburger, Joachim Funke, and Edgar Wunder, eds., *Milieus of Creativity:
An Interdisciplinary Approach to Spatiality of Creativity*, 11–25 Dordrecht, Netherlands: Springer 2009.

Gabora, Liane. "Why the Creative Process Is Not Darwinian: Comment
on 'The Creative Process in Picasso's *Guernica* Sketches: Monotonic
Improvements Versus Nonmonotonic Variants.'" *Creativity Research
Journal* 19, no. 4 (2007): 361–5.

Gaut, Berys. "The Philosophy of Creativity." *Philosophy Compass* 5, no. 12
(2010): 1034–46.

Gilbert, Elizabeth. *Big Magic: Creative Living Beyond Fear.* New York:
Riverhead Books 2015.

Guerra, Vanesa. *La Sombra del Animal: Relatos.* Buenos Aires: Bajo la
Luna 2008.

Hart, Michael Anthony. "Indigenous Worldviews, Knowledge, and
Research: The Development of an Indigenous Research Paradigm."
Journal of Indigenous Voices in Social Work 1, no. 1 (2010): 1–16.

Hemingway, Ernest. *A Moveable Feast.* New York: Scribner 1964.

Hirsch, Edward. *The Demon and the Angel: Searching for the Source of
Artistic Inspiration.* Orlando, FL: Harcourt Books 2002.

Incardona, Juan Diego. *El Campito.* Buenos Aires: Mondadori 2009.

– *Objetos Maravillosos.* Buenos Aires: Tamarisco 2007.

– *Rock Barrial.* Buenos Aires: La Otra Orilla 2010.

– *Villa Celina.* Buenos Aires: Norma 2008.

Kaufman, James C., and John Baer. "The Amusement Park Theory of
Creativity." In Kaufman and Baer, eds., *Creativity across the Domains:
Faces of the Muse*, 321–9 Mahwah, NJ: Lawrence Earbaum Associates
2005.

Kaufman, James C., and Robert J. Sternberg, eds. *The Cambridge Handbook of Creativity.* New York: Cambridge University Press 2010.

Khandwalla, Pradip N. "An Exploratory Investigation of Divergent
Thinking through Protocol Analysis." *Creativity Research Journal* 6, no.
3 (1993): 241–59.

Kofman, Sarah. *Nietzsche and Metaphor.* London: Athlone Press 1993.

Kozbelt, Aaron, Ronald A. Beghetto, and Mark Runco. "Theories of

Creativity." In James C. Kaufman and Robert J. Sternberg, eds., *The Cambridge Handbook of Creativity*, 20–48 New York: Cambridge University Press 2010.

Lionnet, Françoise. *Autobiographical Voices: Race, Gender and Self-Portraiture*. Ithaca, NY: Cornell University Press 1989.

Lispector, Clarice. *A Breath of Life: Pulsations*. Translated by Johnny Lorenz. New York: New Directions 2012.

– *The Hour of the Star*. Translated by Benjamin Moser. New York: New Directions Press 2011.

– *Near to the Wild Heart*. Translated by Alison Entrekin. New York: New Directions 2012.

– *The Passion According to G.H.* Translated by Idra Novay. New York: New Directions 2012.

– *The Stream of Life*. Translated by Elizabeth Lowe and Earl Fitz. Minneapolis: University of Minnesota Press 1989.

Lorca, Federico Garcia. "Theory and Play of the Duende." Translated by A.S. Kline. In *Poetry in Motion*. 2007. http://www.poetryintranslation.com/PITBR/Spanish/LorcaDuende.htm.

Lubart, Todd. "Cross-cultural Perspectives on Creativity." In James C. Kaufman and Robert J. Sternberg, eds., *The Cambridge Handbook of Creativity*, 265–79 New York: Cambridge University Press 2010.

Lubart, Todd, and Robert J. Sternberg. "Creativity: The Individual, the Systems, the Approach." *Creativity Research Journal* 1 (1988): 63–7.

Lumsden, Charles J., and C. Scott Findlay. "Evolution of the Creative Mind." *Creativity Research Journal* 1 (1988): 75–91.

Manguel, Alberto. *The City of Words*. Toronto: Anansi 2007.

Martínez, Guillermo. *Acerca de Roderer*. Buenos Aires: Planeta 1992.

– *Borges y la Matemática*. Buenos Aires: Editorial Seix Barral 2006.

– *Crímenes Imperceptibles*. Buenos Aires: Planeta 2006.

McKerracher, Adrian. "Understanding Creativity, One Metaphor at a Time." *Creativity Research Journal* 28, no. 4 (2016): 416–25. http://www.tandfonline.com/doi/full/10.1080/10400419.2016.1229982.

Merrell, Floyd. "Creation: Algorithmic, Organicist, or Emergent Metaphorical Process?" *Semiotica* 161 (2006): 119–46.

Meusburger, Peter, Joachim Funke, and Edgar Wunder, eds. *Milieus of*

Creativity: An Interdisciplinary Approach to Spatiality of Creativity. Dordrecht, Netherlands: Springer 2009.

Miall, David S. "Metaphor and Transformation: The Problem of Creative Thought." Technical Report #300. Washington, DC: National Institute of Education 1983.

Moran, Seana. "Metaphor Foundations in Creativity Research: Boundary vs. Organism." *Journal of Creative Behavior* 43, no. 1 (2009): 1–22.

Mumford, Michael D., and Michele I. Mobley. "Creativity, Biology, and Culture: Further Comments on Evolution of the Creative Mind." *Creativity Research Journal* 2 (1989): 87–101.

Nakamura, Jeanne, and Mihaly Csikszentmihalyi. "The Concept of Flow." In Charles R. Snyder and Shane J. Lopez, eds., *Handbook of Positive Psychology*, 89–105 New York: Oxford University Press 2002.

Nava, Mica. *Visceral Cosmpolitanism: Gender, Culture and the Normalization of Difference.* Oxford, UK: Berg Publishers 2007.

Nawotka, Edward. "Buenos Aires: 2011 World Book Capital in More Ways Than One." Publishing Perspectives (28 April 2011). http://publishingperspectives.com/2011/04/buenos-aires-world-book-capital/.

Perry, Susan K. "Flow and the Art of Fiction." In James C. Kaufman and John Baer, eds., *Creativity across Domains: Faces of the Muse.* Mahwah, NJ: Lawrence Earlbaum Associates 2005. 23–41.

Pinar, William. *What Is Curriculum Theory?* Mahwah, NJ: Lawrence Erlbaum Associates 2004.

Pinker, Steven. *The Stuff of Thought: Language as a Window into Human Nature.* New York: Viking Press 2007.

Plato. *The Portable Plato.* New York: Viking Press 1948.

Pressfield, Steven. *The War of Art: Break through the Blocks and Win Your Inner Creative Battles.* New York: Rugged Land 2012.

Radman, Zdravko. *Metaphors: Figures of the Mind.* London: Kluwer Academic Publishers 1997.

Richards, Ruth. "Everyday Creativity: Process and Way of Life – Four Key Issues." In James C. Kaufman and Robert J. Sternberg, eds., *The Cambridge Handbook of Creativity*, 189–215 New York: Cambridge University Press 2010.

Ricoeur, Paul. *The Rule of Metaphor: Multi-disciplinary Studies of the Creation of Meaning in Language*. Translated by Robert Czerny. Toronto: University of Toronto Press 1977.

Romero, Simon. "Argentina's New Literary Tradition: Pensions for Aging Writers." New York *Times*, 12 August 2012. http://www.nytimes.com/2012/08/13/world/americas/argentina-offers-its-aging-writers-a-little-security.html.

Rubenson, Daniel L. "Human Capital and the Matthew Effect: Description Does Not Imply Prescription." *Creativity Research Journal* 5, no. 4 (1992): 369–72.

– "On Creativity, Economics, and Baseball." *Creativity Research Journal* 4 (1991): 205–9.

Ruitenberg, Claudia. "Distance and Defamiliarization: Translation as Philosophical Method." *Journal of Philosophy of Education* 43, no. 3 (2009): 421–35.

Sábato, Ernesto. *On Heroes and Tombs*. Translated by Helen R. Lane. Boston: David R Godine 1961/1981.

Simonton, Dean Keith. "The Creative Imagination in Picasso's *Guernica* Sketches: Monotonic Improvements or Nonmonotonic Variants?" *Creativity Research Journal* 19 (2007): 329–44.

– "Quality and Purpose, Quantity and Chance." *Creativity Research Journal* 1 (1988): 68–74.

– "Scientific Creativity as a Combinatorial Process: The Chance Baseline." In Peter Meusburger, Joachim Funke, and Edgar Wunder, eds., *Milieus of Creativity: Knowledge and Space 2*, 39–51 Dordrecht, Netherlands: Springer 2009.

Singer, Irving. *Modes of Creativity: Philosophical Perspectives*. Cambridge, MA: MIT Press 2011.

Sternberg, Robert J. "Domain-generality vs. Domain-specificity of Creativity." In Peter Meusburger, Joachim Funke, and Edgar Wunder, eds., *Milieus of Creativity: An Interdisciplinary Approach to Spatiality of Creativity*, 25–39 Dordrecht, Netherlands: Springer 2009.

Thompson, Robert Farris. *Tango: The Art History of Love*. New York: Pantheon 2005.

Wallas, Graham. *The Art of Thought*. New York: Harcourt Brace 1926.

Weisberg, Robert W. *Creativity: Understanding Innovation in Problem Solving, Science, Invention, and the Arts*. Hoboken, NJ: John Wiley and Sons 2006.

Williams, Emily. "Argentina: A Nation of Off-beat Writers, Exquisite Publishers." *Publishing Perspectives*, 11 October 2010. http://publishingperspectives.com/2010/10/argentina-a-nation-of-offbeat-writers-exquisite-publishers/.

Wilson, Jason. *Buenos Aires: A Cultural and Literary Companion*. New York Interlink Books 2000.

Woolf, Virginia. "A Sketch of the Past." In *Moments of Being*. London: Hogarth Press 1985.

Zwicky, Jan. "Mathematical Analogy and Metaphorical Insight." *For the Learning of Mathematics* 30, no. 1 (2010): 9–14.

– *Wisdom & Metaphor*. Kentville, NS: Gaspereau Press 2003.

Index